Knowing is Seeing!

Create the Magnificent Life You Desire

Wendy Kirkland

About the Book

The goal for *Knowing is Seeing!* is to point each person in the right direction of awareness, heath, abundance, and overall, wholeness, but we can't do it for each other. No one can do it for another person. It's up to each of us to be aware of the path and take the steps ourselves. We've all heard the saying "Seeing is believing". This book illustrates how it is knowing, not just believing, that creates what you see in your reality.

Each day we're provided with opportunities that offer choices to become who we want to be. Moment by moment, life presents us with chances to act and react in ways that are different from our past responses. However, we often find ourselves stuck in a rut, reacting out of habit, unable to make a different choice. So, instead of moving us forward, our personal paths have us traveling in a never-ending circle, where our actions, reactions, and choices lead us nowhere but to where we've already been.

Knowing is Seeing! will put your feet on a different path, recognizing that it's in the present moment that we create our current reality and renew ourselves with revised or updated information and ever-increasing understanding. These moments of conscious awareness can be the first step that puts us on the path to positive change and divine living.

Introduction

You were born deserving. Remind yourself of this fact and expect the very best in each moment. Then, stay in the present moment and enjoy it. The past is gone, and the future is pure imagination. Now is the only true reality. Wallow in it! It is perfect.

Hi, I am Wendy. There are a lot of things I could tell you about myself, but the only thing that matters right now is why I wrote this book and who I wrote it for.

The why is easy to explain. My life has been blessed with abundance, opportunity, adventure, positive relationships, and joy. Yes, there have been moments of loss and grief and worry, but I've always come back to a place of centeredness.

The who is you. The fact that you are reading this this means you were drawn to this book. As I wrote it, I knew there would be people meant to receive its message. With each word as I am thinking about sharing these thoughts, I am thinking about you.

So, this said, let's proceed as friends, where we discuss anything and everything openly, honestly sharing our heartfelt feelings, desires, and understandings. I will be open and honest with you, and you can be the same when you think or express a thought.

Don't Be Afraid to Embrace the Unknown Possibilities

I already know that you want what you have envisioned for yourself. You have plans and goals, some of them heartfelt and, perhaps, divinely inspired, that you want to complete. You want to be happy, successful, and healthy, which is normal and perfectly human. So, when life's events take you to places you don't consciously want to go to, you feel as if something as gone astray, or you made a mistake somewhere along the path.

But really, this is just life's way of taking you to somewhere you need to be or to go for reasons that run deeper than your own understanding. In my day, these were called hard knocks. These trials are designed to open and shed light on your unconscious thoughts and deepen your life experiences.

Often it takes something out of the ordinary or a major shift to wake us up, including you, to shake you loose from "your norm", from ego's grip as it fights to maintain the misguided illusion that "it" is in control. It is this loss of power more than anything else that brings a sense of humility, brings you to search for and see the big picture.

That lack of control reminds you that the key to life–your life–lies in what you do not know. What you do know is a small fraction of the great universal mystery of life and your important part in it. This awareness softens and lightens you, as it helps you release your resistance to this hidden gift. Another gift gleaned from going to these seemingly undesirable places or circumstances is that, in your reaction and response to difficulty, you can see all your patterns and, perhaps, unresolved emotional hang-ups that stand in the way of your unconditional joy and a perfect life.

Joy exists within you whether things are perfect and go your way or not. And, when you search for and don't feel joy, you can still trust that you can find it if you are willing to acknowledge the truth of the situation and move through it.

You can take inspiration from any fairy tale you remember hearing as a kid. A main character lost in a dark forest, frightened and alone. You know that the journey through the woods provides its own level of beauty and authenticity at a deep level. On the other side, they emerge transformed, lighter, braver, and more confident for having traveled though the darkness.

My favorite is Peter Pan.

I plan to briefly share details about my life that I have never talked about or shared with anyone else before, not even family. The reason I am doing so is to openly demonstrate that you are a powerful creator. You have the ability to create the most amazing, wondrous life no matter what has happened previously in your life.

I came across this poem and thought it was too good not to share… the author is Caitriona Loughrey:

> Barely the day started and… it's already six in the evening.
>
> Barely arrived on Monday and its already Friday.
>
> … and the month is already over.
>
> … and the year I almost over.
>
> … and already 40, 50 or 60 years of our lives have passed.
>
> … and we realize that we lost our parents, friends, and we realize it's too late to go back …
>
> So … Let's try, despite everything, to enjoy the remaining time…
>
> Let's keep looking for activities that we like…
>
> Let's put some color in our grey…

Let's smile at the little things in life that put balm in our hearts.

And despite everything, we must continue to enjoy with serenity this time we have left. Let's try to eliminate the *afters.*

I'm doing it after…

I'll say after…

I'll think about it after…

We leave everything for later like "after" is ours.

Because what we don't understand is that:

Afterwards, the coffee gets cold…

afterwards, priorities change…

Afterwards, the charm is broken…

afterwards, health passes…

Afterwards, the kids grow up…

Afterwards, parents get old…

Afterwards… promises are forgotten…

Afterwards… the day becomes the night…

afterwards… life ends

And then it's often too late…

So… Let's leave nothing for later…

Because still waiting to see you later, we can lose the best moments,

the best experiences,

best friends,

the best family…

The day is today… The moment is now…

We are no longer at an age where we can afford to postpone what needs to be done right away.

Yes, You Do Have the Power to Change Your Life

It is commonly believed that it is impossible to make a difference, to improve your life and make the world a better place without unlimited funds, having free time, spending days doing it, or having that type of career, yet most purging, healing, and spreading of joy is accomplished in a matter of minutes. If you believe you can make the world a better place one day at a time, your life and humanity will benefit in countless ways.

Helping the world often takes no more than a positive thought; just a moment projecting a wish for the world is a creative gesture and can be done by the busiest of people. As you're driving your car, think and send out thoughts of joy. This gift you give each day need not be grand or commendable because the positive benefits are the same no matter the literal implications. Do this numerous times a day, you can affect reality, and you can reap the gift of knowing you are improving your life and making the world a better place every single day.

This is the smallest of gestures, perhaps, a beginning step on a life-changing journey, yet its positive impact can be monumental for your life and the world as a whole.

Honest and true, I guarantee that if I can change my life into an unbelievably blessed reality, you can do it, too! Joy is waiting for you!

Are you ready? Let's get started.

Chapter 1

Knowing Is Seeing! Create the Magnificent Life You Desire

Oh, get excited now, because there are more potentials, more possibilities, more opportunities here for you than have ever existed before.

The goal for this book is to point you in the direction of awareness, health, abundance, and overall, wholeness, and inspire you to take that first momentous step. I can't do it for you. No one can do it for another person. It's up to you to become aware of your path and take the steps yourself. No one else can make you "know" anything. Truly, everything must be experienced to be proven it is real to you before it is accepted, so that false perceptions and mistaken beliefs vanish, and wholeness and love can be experienced in the present moment, in your "now."

We've all heard the saying: Seeing is believing. However, my stepfather switched the wording and came up with "Believing is seeing." Eventually, I came up with the words: Knowing is seeing! That's the truth. I say that because there's a huge difference between believing and knowing.

Think of it. To believe something provides its own built-in empty space, an opening to say, "Oops, I goofed and now I've changed my mind." It's been said that unless you know something, you can't accept and experience it.

It's important to understand this right from the start. I didn't write this book to make you believe anything. My goal is to establish a certainty, a knowing that you are already perfect, and you can design and create the life you desire. This book's purpose is to increase your certainty that you already have everything needed to be a perfect-life creator.

Each One of Us is Perfect and Unique

You are unique. Your personality makes you one-of-a-kind, but how did you develop your personal identity? What elements played the most important roles in who you've become? And how can you achieve the wildest, heartfelt life of your dreams?

To answer these questions, let's start with identity. Many theorists have come up with various steps and stages on the path to personality development. Some of the factors involved include genetics, specific life events, as well as emotional, cognitive, social, and moral influences and growth.

We each have a story to tell. You have a story. As you listen to stories about people in the news and on various television shows and media, you might forget that you, too, have a fascinating individual story about where you came from and how you got to the place you are right now in this area and time. You are you, and yet the sheer variety of paths is mind-blowing, from farmers to business execs, inventors to doers (the people who implement and make things happen), homeless people to world travelers, bus drivers to stay-at-home moms, athletes to people who are bedbound.

You're not only unique, you're also interesting. Sometimes, the shy quiet, introverted person has the most amazing life story and the biggest dreams and goals. Two people who have led similar lives in the same location can have vastly different life experiences, leading them to have individual points of view on the same happening. Some people travel a path of wealth, while others struggle, relying on their own meager resources, yet both have one-of-a-kind stories to tell about who they are. Often, they are each truly grateful for the distinctive life circumstances that led them to become the individuals they are. When you take the time to ask questions and listen, you discover endless stories and countless perspectives from which they're told. No two are exactly alike.

Many Journeys, One Mankind

The purpose of life, and the reason you developed a personality in the first place, is to experience what life means and offers, overcome obstacles, make choices, live unselfishly, and share love and do your part by bringing "yourself" to the collective that is all of mankind.

So, let's jump in with both feet. I'm going to continue speaking with you as if we're new friends, who aren't shy, talking comfortably while sitting out on the deck at my home, looking out across a valley with surrounding mountain ranges in the distance.

In other words, no matter who you are, know you are supposed to be here, and let's view ourselves at ease hanging out together.

QUESTIONS TO CONSIDER

1. What is missing in your life right now?
2. What goals or dreams have you carried but never acted on?
3. What makes you special and unique that only you can share with the world?

Chapter 2

Why are You here? What is the point?

Figuring out why you're here is not nearly as important as just honoring the fact that you exist. You are special. You are awesome.

Before I attempt to answer these questions, let me explain why I'm sharing this information with you. I know without a doubt my job or personal objective in this life is to empower you to discover and listen to your own inner voice for specific answers to verify your truth. This discovery is what life is all about for you and me and everyone else.

With certainty, my life and everything I've experienced good, bad, or otherwise has brought me to this point of sharing what I know with you.

We are in this together for our greater awareness and a joy-filled life!

It's often said that life is a journey, and looking at it that way, you can see it's comprised of steps along a path that take you down winding roads of ongoing evolution. Each day you're provided with opportunities that offer choices to become who you want to be. Moment by moment, life presents you with chances to act or react in ways that are different from your past responses. Sounds good, but you can also find yourself stuck in a rut, and you react out of habit, unable to make a different choice. So, instead of moving forward, your personal path has you traveling in a never-ending circle, where your actions, reactions, and choices lead you nowhere but to where you've already been.

Let Go of the Past and Look Forward

When you zero in on your past, it's often difficult to understand how or why you made certain choices or mistakes. This happens because once you learn new information it's tough to reenter the old mental and emotional space you were in before you absorbed the new ideas and facts. For example, you can look back at your parents, and at their child-rearing years. Perhaps back then, spanking and isolating kids were common punishments. Later you wonder how anyone could have thought that was appropriate or even a good idea.

Likewise, at least for most of us, you may look at your past and see it filled with bad choices you can't believe you made. Perhaps, you did things "back then" you'd never do today because you now have information that you didn't have before. Or you weren't able to access the information at that stage of your life. Maya Angelou tried to help people see that some of the things they regretted was lack of knowledge, not ill will.

Our collective human past often reads like a diary of what not to do. Ideas about instructing and disciplining children, being valuable employees, running businesses, treating the environment, or managing mass illness and vaccines like Covid 19, have undergone massive change. In general, understanding takes place the same way that you as an individual become more discerning and thoughtful as you travel your life path. In many ways, this is exactly how it "should" happen. You learn and grow wiser from having experiences, which then help you gather information to help react differently from that point on. You've likely had a few missed opportunities, all-out blunders, and unsuccessful jobs or relationships. But those events possibly taught you about jealous, selfish, or negative tendencies, which in turn gave you chances to gain the personal growth, wisdom, and understanding you have now.

You can live more peacefully with the past knowing that awareness tends to help you do better. Look at it this way, before knowing, you likely do your best. Now, it's true that your limited understanding in that moment might have made your best seem not good enough, but you can at least give your past self the benefit of the doubt. You did your best with what knowledge and understanding you had. You most effectively serve your greater good if you don't dwell on the past, which also means that you stop criticizing yourself.

A far more effective action is to direct your energy and knowledge into your present actions. It's in this present moment that you create your current reality and renew yourself with revised or updated information and ever-increasing understanding. These moments of conscious awareness can be the first step that puts you on the path to positive change. In his novel, *Boy's Life*, Robert R. McCammon stated this clearly:

You know, I do believe in magic. We were born with whirlwinds, forest fires, and comets inside of us. We were born able to sing to birds and read the clouds and see our destiny in grains of sand. But then we get the magic educated right out of our souls. We get it churched out, spanked out, washed out, and combed out. We get put on the straight and narrow and told to be responsible. Told to act our age. Told to grow up for God's sake. And, you know why we were told that? Because the people doing the telling were afraid of our wildness and youth, and because the magic we knew made them ashamed and sad of what they'd allowed within themselves.

Points to Ponder

- You have the power to create the life of your dreams —no one else can do it for you.
- Put aside thoughts, old beliefs, and emotional energy that has led you to feel stuck in your life. Remind yourself that new information is coming your way in this book. Keep reading!
- You have a unique, valuable, and interesting story and everything you need to create the life you want is within you.
- Starting today, shift your thinking in order to absorb and truly understand not only the title of this book, but its premise, its heart: *Knowing is Seeing*!

QUESTIONS TO CONSIDER

1. What past actions or decisions are still weighing you down?
2. What do you need to do to release these burdens from the past?
3. What energizes and excites you when you think about creating a new future for yourself?

Chapter 3

Conscious Awareness

Do you realize your goals and your successes are all about you? Until you begin to dream, there isn't a target. Until you express your desire, there isn't a promise of success. Until you take the first steps, there isn't a direction. Decide what you want and proceed.

Awareness is the point at which you become conscious of being stuck, and you realize what you are doing or not doing. You observe yourself, notice your reactions, actions and choices as if you are watching a stage play about your own life. Awareness is the first step toward change because you can't make a change unless you are aware that a change needs to be made in the first place.

Once you are aware that you want a change, you can then begin to understand why you do what you do. It then becomes difficult not to bring about change (of some kind) because you are no longer asleep to the truth that has guided your behavior and choices. You also begin to realize you are not only the instigator behind the "causes" of your behavior, but you are also the creator of all changes that you now want to take place.

There is a freedom that comes with awareness. Rather than thinking you are stuck in a maze or repetitive cycle where there is no escape, you begin to realize you truly are the play-writer, and you have the lead role in creating your life—not as a reactor, but as an actor. Whether you realize it or not, your reactions and choices are always yours to make. Understanding this is an enormous growth point for many. When you choose to be aware, your past and what is currently present in your life no longer must dictate your future. You are then free to move beyond your self-imposed limits and are allowed to make new choices; it's up to you to take different actions and further expand your understanding. Once you begin the awareness process, your path can't help but bring you forward, paving the way for new experiences that open the door to personal growth and understanding.

Awareness allows you to consciously evolve.

Are you ready? Let's do this! Let's plunge in and expand your understanding of your awareness, including spiritual awareness.

Don't Be Limited by Traditional Definitions

Likely you have a preconceived idea of who or what God is based on what you have been told since you were a child. Then, through this lens, your understanding builds through what you experience, read, digest, and absorb, and it solidifies as your own truth.

Your thoughts are very specific and will create that exact thing as back-up confirmation or verification. Therefore, if you look for God outside of yourself, you won't find it. Your mind and thoughts create what you think and feel God is or should be, but this is a limited, changing concept that you have manufactured.

You are also often swayed by other peoples' beliefs. At least for the moment, you believe you grasp who or what God is; it seems real, until it doesn't. You absorb a fraction of what you think is the truth, and you stop searching since it seems out of the realm of real understanding or proof and needs to be accepted on faith. The truth is you can't find something where it isn't.

Eventually, you likely give up and feel even more confused and perhaps empty because you conclude that knowing God is abstract, beyond proof or certainty.

It is difficult to decide where to start in this personal, yet universal discovery. Do I start with the answer as to who or what God is and how we both fit in, or do I start with the steps to the discovery? Perhaps, the best place to start is at a beginning, like the first words in the Bible, but written as clearly and directly as I can manage.

My personal mental name for God is "One Infinite Creator" or Oneness, yet the name that comes out of my mouth is God, because that's what I've been calling the Creator most of my life. God is Awareness. God is Oneness. God is!

The first words in the Bible are: In the beginning God created the heaven and the earth. And the earth was without form, and void; and darkness was upon the face of the deep.

God creates through thought. There is nothing else, but God. As stated above, in the beginning, God's mind was all that existed. Our physical world didn't exist. It hadn't yet been thought of. God's mind power was all that existed and when there was a thought, that thought was created instantly, and yet the development of that thought creation may have taken what you know as years, centuries, decades, or eons and longer. Instantly is subjective. Its creation happens as soon as it is thought, but formation, evolution, or development takes as long as it takes.

Perhaps, before there were any physical creations, abstracts were thought of, yet these basic concepts could have taken millions or billions of years. Here is a long list of abstract concepts to consider: center and beyond center, right and left, top and bottom or above and below, layers, dimensions, first and next, same, in front of and behind, time, now or then, finite and infinite, in and out, clockwise and counterclockwise, together or apart, bright or dark, heavy or light, long or short, wide or narrow, straight or twisted, stretched or slack, symmetrical or asymmetrical, forward or backward, high, medium or low, vertical, horizontal or circular, leading or behind. I could go on and on. These ideas were only concepts until thoughts of physical creations appeared.

The vastness is mind blowing. To illustrate, let's jump forward from before creation or back from now to September 3, 2003. On that day, the Hubble telescope was in space, and it came to a spot where it became stationary. It focused a telescopic camera on an area that was about a tenth the size of our full moon. If you take our thumb and index finger and put them together so they create a circle and hold it up to the sky, that is about the area of the sky that it focused on. It stayed in place without moving for a little over four months, keeping the camera fixed on the same spot. When it first zeroed in on the spot, the area looked black and empty.

At the end of the photographic period, it produced a camera image that looked like a clear night sky that was full of stars—like looking up at our Milky Way. Each of the glowing dots in the photo is an entire galaxy. Each galaxy contains up to one trillion stars. Each star may have a system of planets. One photo the size of a circle created by your thumb and index finger contains or reveals more than 10,000 galaxies. Imagine what is beyond the stars you see and the rest of the sky surrounding our planet and beyond.

The photo captured galaxies 13 billion light years away, which is the most distant area of space our current technology allows us to photograph. Given the leaps in technology we've seen in our lifetime, what might we see when we leap forward again? One galaxy in the photo contained eight times as many stars as our Milky Way. It is so large it technically shouldn't exist according to current theories in physics.

Whew!

As mentioned, at some point, God thought of physical creations like all those galaxies, and they were projected from thought into existence. God creates through every thought. The heavens, cosmos, galaxies, universe, planets, and earth were and are created, developed, and evolve through thought.

God is all there is, and its essence is a part of everything. It creates from Itself because It is "all there is." A thought from God about the universe, planets, and the earth evolving becomes oceans and eventually dry land, plants and trees, variations happening through weather. Life essence expanding starts in the oceans, and ultimately, it crawls out onto the land to become animals in various forms. Because God is all there is, It is then within all of creation. There isn't yet a definitive answer as to how long this process has taken.

It can't be that God creates anything in which It is not what It is created by and from. Because It is all there is. This is why names for God include Mind or Thought. All of creation, everything that is, is all God. God creates and is aware of Itself in all things. It is what Is. That's why It is also named Creator and Universal Source of Intelligence. Or simply Source.

God is often described as a Single Source Deity, a Duality (male/female) (or Father/Son) or a Trinity - Father, Son and Holy Spirit by various religions.

As I continue and for the purpose of expressing the concepts we are discussing, I am going to divide the overall concept of God into three segments: The "Force" of Love is God, and the "Act" of Loving, expressing Love or creating is God's Love. The third segment is the "Spirit" of God. (So, for my description within this book, there is God, God's Love, and Spirit of God, which is each of us, a personal expression of God.)

God's Love or Love with a capital "L" is what I call the creative aspect of God's universal mind power. It is God expressing love through all that is. This creative thought process or God expressing Itself through thought is God's Love creating, or, said another way, it is the action part of God, creating through Love, like a parent creating a child or an inventor thinking through the concepts of a new project or product.

God's Love is a Universal principle. It has many names. Universal Mind, Cosmic Consciousness, Divine Mind, the Law of Attraction, the Law of Manifestation, the Universal Law of Thought, or the Law of Vibration are a few.

It could be that Mind fits one person's definition of divinity and Creator fits another's, yet the basic concepts might not be so different. Just like if you and I define a good life and abundance, our descriptions might be quite similar and overlap.

To some, an Old Testament God is a benevolent "He," who sits on a throne in some unseen dimension. To others, God is a vengeful ruler, who has guidelines and a set way that things should be done or how life should be lived, and He will inflict punishment to bring you back into line if you stray off course. And still, to other people, God is a more infinite concept, something outside of yourself that you should strive to find, copy, and incorporate within your life. As if you are reaching up to discover and find God, and then draw down those divine aspects to make them your own.

Still others believe each of us, you are spirit or a soul that is attached to God via a string, perhaps, like a silver cord similar to an umbilical cord. You are separate but connected. Others think you are a combination of spirit and soul. Spirit is in your center, your core, surrounded by soul, which is your personal spiritual part, a combination of mind, emotions, and will, and encompassing all this is your outer body. Some version of this may be close to actuality, where Spirit is the God portion or the Holy Spirit or Spirit of God and soul is your individual spiritual aspect.

In the broadest understanding, I suggest you think about the numerous "names" for It: God, One Infinite Creator, Self, Changeless Light, Pure Consciousness, Awareness, Divine Consciousness, Elohim, I Am, Jehovah, Isness, It, Life, the Infinite or Infinity, Being (not human being), Father, Mother, Most High, the Now, Absolute—and more and decide what suits you.

The list could go on to take in the basic concepts in time and space or an infinite number of galaxies, but you get the gist. Whatever you want to call God, It is actually within you. It is who you are.

Rather than God being something outside of yourself that you reach up to or search for to draw down into yourself, I suggest you come to understand that God is who you already are. It isn't as if you are separated like a child whose cord is eventually cut, so it is no longer connected to who created it.

Truly, It is All you are. It is within your body. It has always been there. It is waiting to be discovered, revealed, recognized, and allowed to cast Its influencing light over your physical life, thoughts, reactions, and emotions.

The aspect of God within each of us is the Spirit of God or Holy Spirit. It is the Life Force, Wind, or Breath. It, too, has no beginning or end and existed before creation, yet It dwells in all of creation and is in our hearts, in you and me, and everyone. It is your divine Spirit.

Within God, there is the Universal Source of Intelligence, known as Itself as God; there is God's Love, which is God expressing love through "creative thought." The Spirit of God, the Divine Life Force or Holy Spirit is within you, and each of us, and all creation.

Whew.

I'm taking a deep breath here to explain that I intentionally repeat phrases to help your understanding, but also to be consistent in embedding these concepts through repetition, so, in a sense, the words become affirmations of a new way of thinking about yourself. For your whole life, you have been likely fixated on who you think you are, and it's going to take more than a minute for the information to settle in, get comfortable, and become a knowing of who you truly are. For a while, you will need to be reminded and will need to reconsider and redefine who you know yourself to be and to perhaps, forgive yourself for the lack of recognition.

Okay, off we go.

In simple terms, or as simple as I can manage, let's examine how this all came about. I'll start by saying: God experiences Itself through everything. Everything in existence is all a part of God. At a point in evolution, God thought of human bodies, and they eventually evolved into a vessel in which It could live inside to experience life. All humans, you and each one of us individually, is the spiritual essence of God created through Its thought process of God's Love; each of us is love and spirit residing in human form, a thought creation of God. No separation exists. God is within us, within you through Its Life Force or Spirit; you are God. You are God living a physical life as you.

For simplicity's sake, I am going to use the name God as I write, knowing you understand it includes all three divine aspects (God, God's Love, Spirit of God), unless I think it is important to draw attention to one of the aspects specifically.

The Smithsonian's National Museum of Natural History states in its Human Evolution resources online: Human evolution is the lengthy process of change by which people originated from apelike ancestors. Scientific evidence shows that the physical and behavioral traits shared by all people originated and evolved over a period of approximately six million years.

Eventually, the beginning of agricultural endeavors and the rise of the first civilizations occurred within the past 12,000 years. Families, clans, groups, villages, towns, cities, countries, and race and ethnicity developed over those years into current time.

The earth and all things living on it are and have been projected from the mind or thoughts of God, where Its spiritual essence expands and has created all things over what we understand as extended periods of time. It doesn't have to separate any part of Itself from spiritual mind to be a part of creation or what ultimately evolved into human beings. We are all God and God is all of us, including you!

This can be hard to grasp, and perhaps you will not fully understand and accept the reality of this until you start hearing and talking to God within yourself and recognize that It is not separate from you. It is you and me, and everyone else.

Let me slow down for a minute and step back. So, God is in everything that exists, it is wholly within each creation, so why when it created us as human beings was the process different than all other creations?

Birds, animals, or perhaps, a community of ants might be a good place to start. So, God through the energy of Spirit and focused power of God's Love thought of ants that could live above and below the ground, and they were created and developed through stages of evolution until they became the ants you know now. Ant nests are the physical places where ants live. Anthills are above the underground nests where the workers pile sand or soil outside the entrance to form a mound. A species of ant and all those living within the nest look similar, and most perform the same routine tasks of home building, finding food, producing offspring, and protecting the overall community. It isn't as if each ant is unique in appearance, personality, work ethic, or its life choices, and the way it chooses to experience its life.

All of nature, everything else other than humans, adapts to its environment and tries to remain in its intended setting, until forced to re-acclimate for some reason. Roots from a tree grow around rocks, animals find or build homes in what is available, but overall, their essential life drive remains the same for their particular species.

Imagine that God created human beings and kept our development from expanding in the same way a community of ants has been created. We'd be a different species from other mammals, but, overall, we'd all be the same, evolving in only minor ways to adapt to changing conditions. We'd all find food, build homes, reproduce and have the same overall life objective or drive. God wouldn't have had creative, unique, individual life experiences.

Instead, over six million years, human head size and facial features changed as our brains grew and developed. Our consciousness and drive expanded until humans began to develop more awareness and individuality.

It takes time for the truth of who we are to settle into comfortable acceptance that ants are God's creation, so are elm trees and elephants, and so are we. Eventually, you might ask: If I am God, if we are all God, if we are all made of the same divine essence, then why or how are we all different? Why aren't we like a community of a single species of ants, who are for the most part identical?

Defining Our Own Experience and Interpretation

This brings us to what this is all about for you and me on a personal level. For God to experience human life as you and me, we had to have the opportunity to develop as individuals. How can this happen if we are all created from the same stuff, the same essence of God? When we are conceived and born, we are God. God is all there is, but the Spirit of God within us takes a backseat in a sense. It lays back and quiets Its creative essence and allows our consciousness to develop and, to a modest or focused degree, use thought power of God's Love to create. Our parents, grandparents, and family through life experiences help develop our personalities. For the first three or four years, our personalities form. We are unique, one-of-a-kind. We are the sum total of our bodies that are conceived by two unique people. Where we live, how we are raised, our personal experiences, and emotions originate from this, and then, eventually, we form thoughts that begin to create because that is what thoughts do, they create. About the time of our first memories, God comes forth more actively to experience life through us as unique individuals.

I have a three-year old great-granddaughter. From my new understanding, it's amazing to witness her God purity, free-spirited happiness and the small steps being taken as her personality begins to form. She has foods she likes and those that aren't her favorites. Her imagination is developing. A sense of humor pops up periodically. Her memory is impressive as inquisitiveness blooms. It's fascinating to watch through my Spirit of God witnessing her Spirit of God, letting her personality develop through family experiences. As she enters her third year since birth, she now has twin brothers. Oh, my goodness, to watch her and their fascination of every move she makes is incredible. Truly amazing as I witness from a unique perspective.

God, using God's Love, the creative essence of thought, created us and Its Spirit is within us, within you. You are the divine, living in the material world. God and Its thought power is who you are, but perhaps, you're unaware of Its Spirit presence and the creative essence that is available to you. It's more than just the law for creating or getting what you want. It is intended to be a way of life, where love, joy, and abundance is what you expect and experience because you are drawing what you desire into creation and to you through thought, knowing, and conviction because of who and what you are as an individual personality. To date, these creations, life experiences and your reaction to these events have created your personality and who you are.

Points to Ponder

- Consider the hundreds of names for God and think about what you call God and the image It calls up. Try out different names...Creator, All, Great Spirit, Life Force, The One... to expand your consciousness about the Source of everything, including you.
- God creates within you through Its Life Force, which means you are God. I am God...everything and everyone is God, of God, inseparable from any other part of God.
- Every day remind yourself that God is all there is—and that includes you. If it makes this clearer, think of a trinity: God, God's Love, and the Spirit of God.
- If you find yourself seeking God outside of yourself, slow down, and remember that God is all there is: You are It; It is you.
- Resolve to reread the sections that define, describe, and help you understand that the source of all things is within you.
- Come back to the beginning: *Knowing is Seeing!*

QUESTIONS TO CONSIDER

1. What is something–a change, a feeling of dissatisfaction–that you've recently become aware of?
2. What is your perception of God or a higher power?
3. How does your perception of God or spirituality impact your view of the world and yourself?

Chapter 4

Let's Look at Personalities

Thoughts become things and your voice adds strength to that creation. The more you discuss what you are learning, the more you will incorporate it.

Although we don't know each other well yet, I'd like to highlight a few life-defining moments without embellishing too much and having this read like a memoir or autobiography. My hope is to share that I'm just like everyone else who has had life circumstances to overcome. All of us have had trying, painful, uncomfortable, awkward, and life-defining events that helped form who we have become. I certainly don't want to come across as someone who has had a privileged life with no difficulties. Specific events helped create who I am as an adult and set me on my current path of speaking with you; therefore, I feel compelled to divulge the ugliness and the results as part of the spiritual information I hope to share.

My Unique Personality: Who I Am

My name is Wendy. It is a name I gave myself when I was 16 years old. My birth name was Reyanne, and it never suited me. My father's name was Reyburn, and my mother was Nancy Ann, so a combination of the two names became Reyanne, one name with no middle name.

My dad joined the U.S. Air Force soon after graduating high school and was stationed in California, which was clear across the country from Minnesota where he was born and raised. When he completed boot camp, he returned home for a two-week leave, and my mom advised him she was pregnant with me. He picked her up from her parent's home, and, at 17 years of age, she rode across country with him, and they married along the way.

A month after I was born, I developed a rare condition that supposedly doesn't happen to girls, so it wasn't diagnosed quickly. It's called pyloric stenosis, meaning the valve in the tube leading to the stomach closes and doesn't open again. It closes and creates a floor like a trampoline, causing projectile vomiting (not fun for a new young mother). It went on a long time without diagnosis. Formula changes and varied feeding schedules didn't help. When I was admitted to the hospital, my parents were told to go home and pray.

After surgery and nearly two months in the hospital, my parents took me home. I suspect this troubling time for a young couple and a lack of bonding after birth added to the disconnect that seemed to escalate throughout my early years.

My dad was discharged from the Air Force in 1950, just before the start of the Korean War, and we returned to Minnesota before the birth of my first brother. My parents didn't choose to live near my grandparents, and moved us to Minneapolis, so my dad could attend college. He wanted to study economics and become a professor. Mom did waitress work.

When Dad graduated, we returned to Duluth, where, just like he planned, he took a job as a professor of economics at a local college. They bought a home in a rural area only a few blocks from where my father was raised, which included neighborhood homes, an elementary school, drugstore, a Five and Dime store, an orphanage, and a few other small shops. The area was surrounded by farms that raised dairy cows and horses. In subsequent years, another brother and two sisters came along.

The college offered chances to be socially active and my parents also played golf. My dad became part of a club called the United States Junior Chamber or Jaycees, and he joined Rotary International. These were all typical activities for a professional man and his family during the 1950s and early '60s.

My mom spent several hours a day leisurely soaking in the tub, styling her naturally curly hair, polishing her nails, and applying make-up. She sewed, a skill taught in high school back then, so she followed the trends and made her own dresses, shorts, tops or slacks. I recall hearing people at church or at college gatherings remark that my parents were a handsome couple.

Mom was quick with the belt and hollered whenever we three older children squabbled or made a mess. She liked things neat and tidy. She was relaxed and spoke kindly to me when I'd spend time rubbing lotion on her feet after the younger kids were in bed. Sometimes, she would talk and fuss about her day and how much work kids required.

Mom would also ramble on about her take on life and offer advice. "It's important to be pretty and take time for yourself," she'd say. "You've got to always look your best. When you're older and out in the world, it's going to take you extra time," she rambled. "I applied for a hostess job in a fancy night club. Being pretty brings in big tips."

If I did a good job rubbing her feet, she'd give me a small

Heath candy bar. During these times, Dad often sat at one end of the dining room table grading college students' papers. The other dining room chairs were stacked with copies of the Wall Street Journal that acted as booster seats for different age kids.

When I wasn't busy watching over or entertaining my siblings, I climbed an oak tree behind the garage where I built a treehouse. The huge oak had a special limb that grew from one stem into another. I had to duck under it to enter the nailed-together wood structure. It was the place where my imagination was free. One day the treehouse was a pirate ship, and another day a barn full of animals. I could turn it into a school or an orphanage. Regardless of how I transformed it, it was a safe place to escape to avoid being asked to feed kids, clean up their toys, bathe and dress them, help wipe butts in the bathroom, or be swatted with a belt. I also loved to roam the nearby woods, pick wild raspberries and strawberries, play in the creeks, floating leaf boats with stick and smaller leaf sails, and collecting polished agates.

I missed a lot of school in the first grade from chronic tonsillitis. I fell behind in my studies, especially reading. I was now the oldest of five children and did my share to help entertain my two brothers when my parents were home or when a teenage babysitter looked after the baby and next youngest kid. Life overall seemed normal for a big family in that era. There were exceptions, though. My parents often remarked that I wasn't as smart as my younger brothers. I had buckteeth from years of thumb sucking and a couple moles on my face, so I wasn't considered nearly as cute as my younger sisters.

I fell further behind in school every year. One day, my third-grade teacher wrote the word "THEN" on the chalkboard and asked me to stand and read the word. I did my best to sound it out. "TH -th- an," I guessed. She then wrote "THAN" on the board next to it and went back and forth between the two.

Correcting me and expecting me to say the next one. Back and forth, she went. The other kids laughed and taunted me: "Mole face doesn't know the difference between then and than." "Back to the first grade you go." "She's not just ugly, she's stupid." "Holy Moly!"

I ran from the classroom and out of the school, sobbing and choking as I darted between houses until I reached my treehouse.

The next Saturday, my family had a picnic on an outside table in the side yard. I was cutting up a hotdog for one of my younger sisters, and my brother jabbed me in the ribs with his elbow. "I hate that our names are almost the same, Reyburn and Reyanne. The kids tease me." My brother was Reyburn Junior. "They say Rey-Rey means stupid and ugly. It is all because of you. I wish my name was different."

My dad came off the picnic bench and knocked my brother over and he fell backwards and hit the ground. He grabbed him by the shoulders and shook him, "You be proud of your name. It is my name!"

I tried to wedge myself between my dad and younger brother, "He didn't mean it. He was just teasing me because I'm different. "I'm …" I bit my tongue so my dad's wrath wouldn't turn to me if I implied, I was ugly or dumb.

It was easy to see why I didn't quite fit: My mom liked pretty people, and my dad liked intelligent ones. The smartest college students often came to the house to play chess or cribbage on the weekends with my dad, while Mom served lemonade, leaned in close to the students, and flitted around the room like the women pictured in the Vogue magazines she often read.

One day, during the summer, when I was 10 years old, I wandered into the local Five and Dime store. I often strolled through the aisles looking at nail polish and the few toys on the shelves. "Hi there, pretty girl," a man called from behind the counter. "Good afternoon." I looked around, not realizing he was talking to me. I was the only one in the store.

"Hi," I said.

"It's been quiet today. It's nice to have such a pretty girl come in," he said, grinning.

I rushed from the store. No one in my life, ever, referred to me as pretty. I went back to the store the next day, and, as the man rang up and bagged a lady's purchase, he smiled at me and nodded hello.

I returned the following day, and he spotted me and said, "Well, well, if you aren't the prettiest girl, I've seen all day."

I meandered up and down the narrow aisles and lifted a bottle of nail polish. "How much is this color nail polish?" I asked.

He came closer. "Fifty-nine cents."

"I'll come get it tomorrow," I said as I strolled away from where he was standing. I tried to guess how old he was, perhaps about my dad's age, maybe thirty.

Following me, he asked, "What's your favorite thing in the store?"

I didn't have to think hard because I often admired a cowboy hat, perched high on a top shelf display. "The cowboy hat."

"This one?" I nodded and he handed it to me. I brushed my hand across the felt brim.

"Put it on. Let's see how it looks."

I did as he asked and put the hat on.

"Oh, my. Now there is a beautiful cowgirl if I ever saw one."

My face burned from sudden blushing. I removed the hat and headed to the door.

"What's your name?" he asked.

"Reyanne."

"Reyanne, come back tomorrow, and we'll discuss how you can go home with that hat."

The next day I went into the store to buy the nail polish with leftover birthday money. Someone else was working, and the man wasn't there. I remember feeling disappointed. When he smiled at me, it made me feel good. He thought I was pretty.

One day, the next week, I went into the store. "Well, hello again," the man said. "I've missed seeing you. Every time I look at that hat, I think of you." He slowly walked closer, straightening items on the shelves as he approached. "On Monday, I told a lady that the hat didn't suit her, so she wouldn't buy it. It looked so good on you."

"I don't have the money to buy it." I looked up to its perch high on the shelf. "My birthday isn't 'til January."

"Maybe there's another way for you to earn the cowboy hat."

"I could work for it. I could help dust or straighten the shelves." I lined up a row of toothpaste boxes to show him.

"I have an even better idea." He stepped closer to where I was fiddling around with bottles of Listerine. "If you come into the store fifteen times and let me touch your girl parts, the hat is yours." I'm sure my face showed a lack of understanding. "Like this." He slowly slid his hand softly between my legs and gently moved his fingers. "It feels good, doesn't it?"

I didn't know what to think. It didn't hurt. It kind of tickled.

"Fifteen visits," he said. "We'll say this is the first one." I wiggled and went to take a step. "Just stand still. It doesn't take long." He stood behind me, moved a bit closer and made grunting noises like my grandpa made when he was enjoying his bowl of Jell-o with fruit cocktail mixed in.

I straightened another row of bottles as his arm draped around my waist and between my legs.

"Uhh," he moaned. "One down, pretty girl. Fourteen more and the hat is yours."

By the fifth visit, he was slipping his hands into my shorts. Sometimes, it hurt. On the ninth time, when I entered the store, there was another man behind the counter. The cowboy hat sat high on the shelf. "You're new," I said as I straightened the nail polish bottles, lining up the colors.

"First day," he said as he read something behind the counter. He never really looked up at me. "Other fellow quit."

I had no reason to go back to the Five and Dime.

A few months after this incident, I discovered there was some question about my parentage. In the attic, I found a letter a man wrote to my mother years earlier. He claimed he was my father. I sat with the information for a couple weeks, upset and not knowing what to think. I learned Reyburn had doubts, too. "We'll never know for sure," my dad said when I got up the nerve to ask him. "It might explain why you have straight light hair and look different."

One day, I found my mom's old yearbook and looked up the name of the boy who wrote the letter. I didn't think I looked like him either.

"I was very popular," my mom said one night as I rubbed her feet and had asked her who she thought my father was. My mother evidently had relationships with several boyfriends. "I'm sure your dad is your father. It doesn't matter anyway; he is your dad in every way that counts."

Since I struggled at the neighborhood school, my parents sent me to an elementary school associated with the college for my sixth and seventh grades. I had summer classes to help me reach a passable level and advance to the next class. The new school was part of the college where my dad taught economics. I rode to school with him each morning, hung out at the college after school, and then rode home with him in the afternoon. I enjoyed the one-on-one time with my dad. The college also gave students studying to become teachers the opportunity for practice teaching, so we had one main teacher and several student aides.

When I was twelve years old, and two months into my

seventh-grade year, my parents separated without any warning and no explanation. Apparently, my mother had become involved with someone, a man I knew only as a casual visitor in our home—someone I'd have called a family friend.

Suddenly, on Halloween day, without being told what was going on, my four siblings and I boarded a plane bound for Florida and our new home. We were one family living in Duluth, Minnesota one day, and a new family in Florida the next. No explanation for the next nine months. This move involved a lot of change. New environment, new home, crazy weather change, and even the air smelled different. We had no close extended family, new schools, new friends, a new man pretending to be a parent. No sign of our dad.

It turned out my dad moved to New York City and worked for a book publisher. The summer after we moved, Mom put me on a plane to New York for a week-long visit with him. "They have awesome cosmetic stores in New York, bring me back a red lipstick from Nordstrom's," she called as I handed the flight attendant my ticket.

Earlier in the day, my stepfather Abbott had slipped me two twenty-dollar bills and two fives. "Shh, it's our secret. Just in case you need it or see something nice."

The plane landed at 7:15 pm, but I wandered around the airport wondering where I was supposed to go because it took a while for my dad to show up. We rode a cab to the place he lived.

My dad had to work the day after my arrival. I had my own small hotel room. My dad's room was down the hall. I am calling it a hotel, yet it was where he lived all the time in a non-fancy basic bedroom with a bathroom—an apartment hotel, really. He came and checked on me about 7:00 AM and said he would be back at 5:00 PM. He gave me some money to buy something to eat and told me not to wander too far away.

I strolled around New York City while he worked. After

lunch, I went to a hair salon and got my hair done without an appointment by a male stylist. So weird. I was tall for my age and perhaps looked older than thirteen. The stylist invited me into the back room to see a tattoo he recently had done on his lower belly. I paid at the desk and slipped out after asking the girl where Nordstrom's was and without seeing the stylist's tattoo. Besides, he wasn't very cute.

A makeup artist at Nordstrom's applied foundation, blush, eyeshadow and mascara to my teenage face. Suddenly, I looked ten years older. I bought my mom's lipstick and walked the city, wearing a light tweed navy blue checked mini-skirt and matching jacket.

I went back to the hotel by 5:00 PM, and when my dad arrived home, he was taken aback by my appearance. He must have forgotten how old I really was because after eating dinner, he took me to several bars. In the Peppermint Lounge, I sipped a Manhattan and watched dancers do the Twist.

On Saturday, we went to Greenwich Village and went to what he called a flop house. There were lots of people, music, and dancing. The room was so full of smoke it was hard to breathe. My dad knew a few of the people, and I was introduced as a friend from Florida, not as his daughter.

My dad tapped on my door Sunday morning. I was dressed and ready. I had put a little of the lipstick I bought Mom on my lips and rubbed a smudge on my cheeks. On the cab ride home the night before, Dad mentioned the Adventure Land amusement park. "Are you ready?" he asked when I opened the door.

"Not exactly." I moved to a chair as he walked in. "What happened between you and Mom?" I asked, sitting down. "Why are you here, and we are there? I hate Abbott. Life is so different. Florida is hot. It's weird to see Negro people. I never saw one before. They have separate bathrooms. Why is that? Paris, our Negro maid is super nice. I don't get the difference, and I don't like school there." I babbled like I had exploded. "But it seems like compared to Minnesota kids, I'm smarter. What happened? Don't you love Mom anymore? Why aren't you in Florida with us?"

He plopped onto the bed, and I leaned forward in my chair. "Your mom met Abbott at the club where she worked. She mentioned that he was a big tipper, and he flirted with her."

He paused before saying, "I probably shouldn't be telling you this, but you're probably old enough." He sat for a minute as if considering his words. "I like to watch." He ran his hands through his wavy hair. "I suggested that she flirt with him and invite him to the house when you kids were in school. They would have sex, and I would be in the closet watching. I like to watch."

"You watch?"

"It's how I get aroused." He stroked his chin. "Jesus, it started when I was your age. About thirteen. When my dad got mad at me, he shut me away in the closet under the stairway at our house."

"At Gaga's house," I asked, knowing my grandmother's house well.

He nodded, "He'd put me in there and tell me not to come out until he told me to. I'd cry, and he told me to shut the fuck up. One time, I picked up a swimmer's rubber bathing cap that was in a box on the floor and pushed it against my face so he wouldn't hear me crying. I sobbed into it. The rubber of the hat had an unusual smell. That was the first time I remember becoming sexually aroused.

"I know it is weird." He rubbed his forehead. "If I see a tire inner tube on the side of the road, sometimes, I stop and pick it up because it has a similar smell. I like to be in the closet, smell the rubber, touch myself, and watch.

"Your mom ended up falling in love with Abbott, and they

decided to move away. To start over. When the divorce is final, I imagine they will get married."

I didn't know what to say. Divorce? I knew Abbott had a son in Minnesota. I thought of Abbott as a family friend who was hanging out with us for a while, giving him time to open a furniture store. I saw him as someone who pretended to be a dad once in a while. Abbott and Mom had separate bedrooms—or I thought they did. I was numb.

Divorce was easier to wrap my brain around than sex and a rubber swim cap.

"I never met your dad," I said. "He died, right?" My dad's sister, her husband, and three kids, my cousins, lived with my grandmother, Gaga. I never really thought much about my dad's father since I'd never seen him or heard him mentioned much.

"He committed suicide when I was fourteen," my dad said, getting to his feet. "He did it in a hotel just like this. Are you ready for breakfast and the amusement park?"

Conversation over.

I flew home to Florida two days later. As I stared out the window, I thought about everything I had learned about my dad and the upcoming divorce. "You must like to do more than watch," I said to myself. "You produced four or maybe five kids."

Later that fall, I started the eighth grade and, before long, I became sexually active with my first boyfriend. I was a full-on, blooming teenager. I loved going to Friday night dances on the beach boardwalk. One Friday, I complained to my mom, "Damn, if I have to watch the kids, I won't be able to go to the dance. It's not fair. Geez, you're lazy."

Mom left my room and came back with a wide belt. She started hitting me with it. I knew how to turn and crouch so she just hit my backside. Through the years, I developed this technique. "This is for talking bad and stealing money from your sister's piggy bank." One end of the belt slipped from her hand

and the buckle flew around my waist and tore open my belly button so that it gushed blood.

Not long after, maybe two months into the eighth grade, I was sent away to a private school, several hundred miles away from where my family lived. I assumed I was sent away because I was too much trouble. That might have been so, but at least I didn't have to watch and clean up after four kids.

I attended the school for a year and a summer without returning home. It was what I have since learned was a private "reform" school. I got a phone call from mom every couple of weeks on a payphone to check to see how I was doing.

A violent event happened one night at the school when the housemother let the seniors take charge. Late into the night, the senior girls took each student back into the laundry area. One of them threatened to place a hot clothes iron against the girls' faces. The only way we could keep this from happening was if we admitted we'd stolen something out of another kid's room.

When a girl came at me with the iron, I shoved her so hard that she flipped back and over one of the ironing boards screwed to the wall. The iron fell and scorched her leg. I was scared. I was ugly enough with a mouth full of braces on my upper and lower teeth and with two moles on my face, I didn't need a burn scar. The senior girl screamed as if she was being murdered, and the housemother came running.

The next morning, I ran away, not out of guilt, but fear. Again, I just didn't fit in. I walked country roads located hundreds of miles away from my family. Finally, someone offered me a ride, gave me money for a Greyhound bus ticket. I slept in a chair in the bus station until the bus left Orlando to Jacksonville Beach late in the night.

The bus arrived about noon, and I walked a mile or so home. There was a car I didn't recognize in the driveway and a man I didn't know mowing the yard. I returned to find my family had moved from our rental house. Other people lived in what I thought was our home, and they had no idea where my family had moved. "Come into the house, and I'll help you figure this out," the man said. I took off running.

I ran down the street for a couple blocks and into the swamp area where I had often fished for blue-shell crabs with chicken necks tied to strings. I sobbed. I couldn't believe my mom and Abbott moved without telling me. I couldn't think what to do next. I didn't have a clue where my family lived. I wasn't going to go back to the school and wait for a phone call. Besides, I didn't have enough money for another pricey bus ticket. I leaned against the base of a palm and sank to the sandy ground. I cried so deeply my stomach knotted. I choked and coughed with the dry heaves. I hadn't eaten in a day and a half.

Finally, I realized I knew the name of the furniture store Abbott had opened after we moved from Minnesota. I peed in the woods, washed my face with swamp water and walked back to the main street. I rode several city buses from the small beach town into Jacksonville, asking directions along the way.

My parents, meaning Mom and Abbott, had been advised I had run away, but were surprised when I showed up at the store. They called the police to call off the search in the country town where the school was located. Of course, I was in trouble for leaving school and wasting the money paid toward tuition.

"If you send me away again, I'll run away, so you might as well save your money," I insisted. I wasn't kidding.

My parents went to the school to pick up the clothes and personal things I'd left behind. When they returned home, they related the details of an event that took place. "We gathered your things and noticed your transistor radio was missing. We asked a couple girls about it, and they thought they knew where it was," Mom said. "The girls took off, and when they came back, they had the radio. Then a girl came stumbling out of a room crying, her mouth bloody and a tooth missing. One of the girls had punched her."

My mom shook her head and walked into the kitchen to start dinner. "That place cost us a lot of money, and that girl's parents will pay a pretty penny to get her tooth fixed. We know about costly dental bills."

Their new rental house was small. It was a temporary place while the new house with a pool that Abbott designed was being built. I slept in the front screened porch on a folding cot bed. I had to pull the bed into the center of the porch when it rained, so I didn't get splashed.

Eventually, we moved into the new house, and I did my best to fit in and not cause trouble. I hadn't seen my dad since my New York trip. He just dropped out of my life. Mom mentioned he had moved to South Florida and had also gotten married and was expecting a child.

Abbott thought that as the first teenager in the family, I should go see a psychiatrist. He made the appointments for me, and I went to see a man every other week. He asked tons of questions. What makes you sad? Happy? Anything different this week? What do you dream about? It all seemed pretty silly to me. I started making up wild stories to keep him entertained for the hour appointment. He actively took notes about naked elves that climbed in and around the school bus that only I could see. I told him I'd dreamed of being in a fishing boat accident that left me stranded on an island, where I managed alone by eating crabs and bananas.

Before the sixth appointment, Abbott told me I didn't need to go anymore. The doctor had committed suicide. He'd come across as an odd man, but at the time, I hoped his decision to end his life wasn't based on the made-up stories I told.

In Minnesota, I had been raised Christian, attending one of the churches close to our home, sometimes Lutheran, but primarily a Presbyterian Sunday school. My new stepfather, Abbott, was Jewish. They enrolled me in weekly classes to learn about Judaism. Attending this class caused problems because I asked questions that related to my earlier Christian education. In truth, the class was designed to be more like formal education for Jewish kids, not a conversion class to become a Jew. I tried to make friends with the other teenagers. The girls didn't like me because I was competition for the boys' attention, and, though the boys may have been interested in "the new girl," I couldn't be considered as a girlfriend because I wasn't Jewish in the first place, although Mom and Abbott didn't have that barrier between them.

My twin siblings were born when I was sixteen and in tenth grade. So now we were now seven children. It was quite a bonus having me around to help with the newborns.

During this time, I chose my own name: Wendy. Of course, I chose Wendy because in Peter Pan, Wendy Darling was the mother of the lost boys. I was lost, too.

The black and white version of "Peter Pan" was first televised in 1956, so I was eight years old the first time I saw it, the second being a colorized version in 1960. In researching now as an adult, it seems the name was created by J. M. Barrie, the author of Peter Pan. Although my family didn't have a TV yet in 1956, "Peter Pan" was my first television experience, so I likely saw it at a neighbor's house. I recall watching TV shows now and again with our neighbors.

When I went to a new school in 1964, I started introducing myself as Wendy and telling more or less everyone I ran into my name was Wendy. It didn't take long before my parents and grandparents also started called me Wendy. I think they just figured it wasn't worth arguing about. It caused confusion later in life when my driver's license (obtained through my high school drivers-ed class) stated I was Wendy, yet my birth certificate listed

Reyanne. Having two names created an awkward mess for a lot of years.

During the summer between the eleventh and twelfth grade, I created a fantasy job. I told my mom and Abbott I had been hired by an advertising agency to file papers, answer the phone, and paste up ads. It was all a lie. Inside I felt resentful. Helping to take care of two-year-old twins and two middle school kids wasn't how I wanted to spend the summer.

I got on a bus in the morning and went downtown and wandered around, read a book, looked in department stores, talked to wait staff during lunch, and just hung out. Some days I went over to a girlfriend's house. My friend actually had a job and her mom, who felt sorry for me, let me take two- or three-hour naps in my friend's room. I'm sure I exaggerated how tired I was from bathing two-year-olds and getting up at night with them because their cribs were right next to my room at my end of the hall.

One of my boyfriends, and I had several, was in the Navy and periodically sent a few dollars to put aside for our future. This extra cash provided bus fare and lunch money to keep up my ruse. At the time, I probably collected boyfriends to prove I was pretty enough to have someone care about me.

After about two months, the truth came out. My mom called the advertising agency and asked to speak with me, and, of course, they had never heard of me. I had no choice but to own up to my deceit.

It was during these high school and later teen years that I began my search for who I really was. As you can see from what came before, I didn't feel like I fit who or what I was supposed to be. I was the oldest of five children thought to be conceived by Reyburn (maybe) and Nancy, who I had known to be my parents. Then, I acquired my half-sister twins conceived by Abbott and Nancy. I also had Abbott's son Leslie, my stepbrother; I met him twice and we kissed a couple times as if we weren't related. Plus, another half-sibling conceived between Reyburn and a woman I'd never met. She had five other children from her previous marriage, and they lived with their dad across the country.

I graduated high school in 1966, the year the schools integrated in Florida, meaning African American and white students attended the same schools. Within a couple months of graduating, I eloped with my boyfriend Jack, who was as big a mess as I was. He had joined the Air Force during the Vietnam War right out of high school. Within a few months, we found out I was pregnant with our first child.

Life started to repeat itself.

During those first years of marriage, I spent a lot of one-on-one time with our daughter. Some people probably would have described me as a child raising a child. Not really. By then I'd learned that painful situations come and go. Each episode is just a component within the grand cycle of life. When we choose to experience it as just a small puzzle piece, pain can then serve as an important teacher, and often it just fades away. That was how I chose to handle stress. I did what had to be done and let it dissipate and float away like an evening fog.

I came to understand that when our pain becomes imbedded, it's detrimental to who we are, our well-being, development, and mental outlook. If we take time to notice that we feel closed off, resentful, heavy-hearted, or we hide to avoid being hurt again, we may discover a part of us is still actually stuck in the pain, and it periodically rises to be experienced again and again.

Much of my first twenty-five years felt like it was locked in a quick rinse and repeat cycle. Jack and I we were forever searching for the next "better thing" -- jobs, apartment, furniture and decorations. It was mostly just us, we seldom let anyone else get too close. No life-long friends.

We all get trapped in our feelings for many reasons.

As a child, it's natural to cry, throw a fit, and then, just let the experience move through you. Often, you see children laugh, cry, and laugh again within a short period of time. Each emotion is expressed, and then, the next experience fills the emptied space. By acknowledging your pain in this way, your emotions wash you clean, leaving you open and available to new experiences.

As you develop, you often decide that expressing your feelings is no longer appropriate, and you develop coping skills to deal with pain and discomfort. Because you find your feelings—or expressions of them—unacceptable, you may learn it's smarter in your environment to hide your emotions by stuffing them down. Or you run away from them, acting as if they never happened. At other times, you begin thinking that if only you stay isolated and closed off, and don't dare to venture out to try new things, you can keep ourselves safe from pain, disappointment, or rejection. It's possible that you became accustomed to pain, and adapted to it, so much so, the thought of being without the pain scares you even more. It's important to discover how you handle pain because, if you continue to hold onto it, you expend a lot of energy that could flow into creating more positive experiences.

For various reasons, Jack and I were two lost people, even broken in some ways, and we responded to our circumstances in different ways. I'd often exaggerate my conscious efforts to remain peppy and upbeat most of the time. That could be so annoying to Jack, who was more of a sour person and easily irritated. He was humorous and friendly with strangers, as if conditioned to be that way, but was easily bugged by family and those close to him. He was giving in to emotional troubles, while I tried to ignore them by "rising above."

At any point, over the next forty years, I have claimed that my early life experiences, which I seldom dwelled on and haven't talked about, taught me to be strong, resilient, and resourceful woman. That's the way I saw myself but didn't realize there were lingering effects of the past "hanging around."

In this section, I mentioned these events to show that at the time, I was indeed lost. Jack and I were lost, perhaps, broken. I didn't have a clear view of who Wendy was. I had limited ability to value myself. But I had a persistent inner drive to search for the answers and eventually, I figured out who I was…am. Even better, I learned who we all are!

When we started discussing personalities, I said I'd share life details that helped define who I have become as an adult. I also describe how the details in my life put me on this spiritual journey. Ultimately, it was the path that led me to sharing with you who we truly are as God.

For years, I identified with an internal desire, a state of mind that fueled my ongoing search to discover what life is all about. Life beyond a struggle through difficulties that seem to be tossed arbitrarily into my path.

So, as any philosopher of old and modern psychologists will agree, it's abundantly clear that life events and personal decisions create and design our individual personalities and influence other ongoing life choices, which then influence…and so on. Life questions are often not about the facts of influences and effects, but rather, about process. That's what I was looking for when I read books, asked questions, and attended a variety of churches, searching for the answers. I see now that the answers to my questions were there within me all the time, but my personality, or who I thought I was, based on the life I had lived, did a good job of concealing the answers from me.

So, for all of us, it comes down to reaching inside—and this book is about making those discoveries.

Your Unique Personality: Who You Are

Before moving on, take a few minutes or whatever time you need to think about and unveil the major episodes in your life that were part of forming your personality. The events or occurrences certainly don't have to be negative or hurtful. Joyous events, moments of growth, or recognition can be equally formative.

Dig deep, look for events and happenings that helped define who you have become, so that, if needed, you can learn how to zero in on who you truly are and how to capitalize on that strength and creative ability.

1. Think about or make a list of the best memories you have and the people, places and things that comprise those memories. Think of the way they helped shape and reinforce your strengths and the qualities you want to continue to develop.

2. Identify events that shaped you, but do not call up great memories, or perhaps have caused you to conceal who you really are.

3. Resolve to zero in on who you truly are and learn how to capitalize on those strengths and creative abilities.

Life Unfolds

With this new understanding, it's fascinating to look back at the decisions or choices you made as you created your individual life. You can also learn from looking at the lives of others you're close to or have been in the past. When I look at events flying by during my early adult years, I see changes and some tragedy, and a lot of searching to see what fit and what didn't.

Abbott's son, Leslie, was in the Army at the same time my husband Jack was in the Air Force. Leslie sustained two injuries where he was shot in Vietnam, recovered, and went back on duty. Tragically, he died from a third shooting in 1968.

I mention this because when Jack's Air Force service was over and he was discharged unharmed, we moved to South Florida where my dad, Reyburn, lived with his second wife, my new stepmother, and their daughter. Jack attended the college where my dad was on the faculty and studied horticulture and landscape design.

During his two years at the college, he also worked part-time collecting water and plant specimens from the Everglades and doing laboratory testing. Then Abbott offered Jack a job selling furniture wholesale to furniture stores.

Abbott's furniture store in Jacksonville, the one I remembered and located in order to find my family, had burned down. Questions arose about how the fire started, but nothing negative against Abbott was ever proven. Having been involved in furniture sales all his life, Abbott was now a sales representative for several furniture manufacturers. His job involved travel, and he assigned Jack to cover South Florida, while Abbott sold to the northern half of the state.

My brother, Reyburn (Bob) had been an honor student throughout school. It came easy for him. He took after my dad and being smart was his driving force. Earlier in the twelfth grade, he actively researched and studied drugs like it was a hobby. He didn't partake; he studied. He graduated college magna cum laude, earning an accounting degree, and took a job with the Internal Revenue Service. He was handsome, but shy and uncomfortable around people. He, too, moved to South Florida, close to where our dad lived. (My family was among the millions of people moving from the northern part of the country to Florida, which was in a growth spurt during these years.)

A couple years later, when our first daughter was six years old, I became pregnant with our second child. It was during this time that my youngest brother Jeffrey (Jeff) a free spirit, attended college, and, during his freshman year, had a mild motor scooter accident. The girl on the back of the scooter had a scratch on her nose from going over the side of the road and onto a grassy embankment. Jeff landed funny, suffered a broken back, and became a paraplegic from the mid-chest down at age 20.

After a long hospital stay, he switched his college major to psychology. Before long, he married. He made special arrangements to have innovative leg braces made so that he could stand during the service, and then, carefully and with a great deal of effort, walk down the aisle with his bride.

Jeff graduated college, and, before long, he developed a program for the State of Georgia for para- and quadriplegics and became the director of an institute for rehabilitation, instruction, and therapy with the goal of independent living.

Jack and I and the two girls gradually made our way back to Jacksonville with a two-year pit-stop midway in Lakeland, Florida. We both worked for Abbott in another new business, a wholesale furniture construction plant that he and a business partner started called Comf-vertible, which made sofa hide-a-beds.

Soon after we moved back to Jacksonville, I learned I was pregnant with our third child, six years between each of them. Jack formed his own business, Lawn Saver, a lawn irrigation company that also offered lawn maintenance, and I opened a gift shop in the front of his business. He parked vehicles and stored equipment in the back fenced area of the building, and I sold out of the front.

I started making my version of Cabbage Patch dolls, hiring other women to help make the bodies, and I did the facial details and dressed them. The dolls were displayed in cute settings like dolls in a bathtub with Styrofoam bubbles and on swings. They did cartwheels, napped, or sat together playing Monopoly. I sold hundreds of dolls during the holidays out of the store named after the dolls, Peppermint Pals. I also sold other handcrafted items on consignment.

Life settled into a comfortable and perhaps routine living situation.

During this time, my brother Bob (Reyburn Jr.), who still lived in South Florida, died at age 33 of a drug overdose. It was difficult to understand how it could have happened. Of the seven kids, he had the greatest intellect and educational potential.

Over time, I realized that each of us has the opportunity to use, adjust, or ignore what life hands out based on what we have created through our thoughts, beliefs, and knowing. Truly, during each moment, we have the ability to create what we want our lives to be. The choices are personal and unending.

Clothed in Your Personality

Talk about unending. I recently read an article that explained science has proven there are three billion parts within one molecule of DNA. DNA is a storage system, a remembrance system that holds layers upon layers of information. Biological, life lessons, and activation are the three higher DNA growth levels.

Before the rapid accumulation of information about the brain, most of us had no idea that the heart has 40,000 sensory neurons involved in relaying ascending information to the brain. The heart forms and starts beating in a fetus before the brain begins to develop. The heart emits an electric field that changes according to our emotions and sends more information to the brain than the brain sends to the heart. Heart rhythms help the brain in creating and in innovative problem solving. Based on

God using Its Love to create, it's logical that the heart would be the initiator of brain waves.

Information beyond this becomes a blur for me as my goal is to understand how to use and apply this new understanding about God being us and, in our lives, right now, day in and day out, rather than decoding the mysteries of the science behind the human body. That said, the idea of God thinking through and creating all the elements in nature and, in the human body, and for it to have the means to function as an individual, you and me, or my siblings is unfathomable. Whew—40,000 sensory neurons. This is all as varied and complex as the universe and galaxies. That said, in many ways, the vastness seems comparable.

God is what It is. Yet, It wants to "be," to be heard, to experience and to be experienced. God wants to have individual experiences and for individuals to experience It. To have a personality as a veil is the only way for God to have individual experiences. Without our personalities, God would be and have only Its oneness, Its knowing of Its completeness of and in spiritual and physical worlds. It is everything, and yet Its wholeness limits the physical experiences God can have and feel.

The bottom line is you and I are God clothed in our personalities. Because you are God, you are a creator. Every thought you have creates because you are God, and God creates through every thought. Likely you are not aware of this reality, because it is more typical to see yourself as separate from the Creator. Where you think stuff just happens to you randomly.

Likely, you look at the outside world and find it in a state of seeming chaos and disorder. You could feel compelled to change or fix the situation from one of confusion into one of peace, yet you may be often disappointed by your best attempts, because your thoughts are a jumble of hope and disappointment. Or, put another way, one negating the other. One reason for your confusion rests in the principle that you cannot bring to the world what you don't understand or have the means to offer. You have to discover and recognize it within yourself first. This is what the old saying, "You can't give what you don't have," comes down to.

Peace and positive creations start in your own mind and heart, not outside of yourself; until its roots are firmly embedded within you, you cannot manifest it externally or bring it into your own life. Once you find it within, you can then share it with your family, your community, and the whole world. You may already be doing that, but for most of us, the first step is looking within and honestly evaluating the state of our own awareness and connection to God.

This is it, the one truth, the one law: God is all there is, and God creates through thought. This means that every thought God has, and therefore, every thought you have, since God is within you, creates precisely. Every thought, no exception! Think about it, there is nothing that has been created in the physical world that wasn't first created in the mind.

Your life, that which you are, all the physical things that surround you and the life you lead are manifestations of human thought, God's thoughts through you.

So, you and I create our lives and our world through our thoughts, which when multiplied become beliefs and, perhaps, eventually, knowing. The power that has built galaxies flows through our veins, through your veins. You are a living, breathing embodiment of God. You have become what you know, who you trust and believe, and that all starts in your heart and mind.

Points to Ponder

- God creates through Its thoughts; since you and God are one, you create through your thoughts.

- Your personality is an individual expression of God's desire to create experiences and for It to be experienced.
- Since you are God and God is you, your life is your creation, arising from your thoughts and fueled by desires and conscious direction.
- Remind yourself as often as necessary that you are not separate from God and everything in the Universe, but one with all that is.

QUESTIONS TO CONSIDER

1. What three details do you think are important for people to know about you?
2. When people describe your personality, what kind of words or phrases do they use? Does your perception match theirs?
3. What facets of your personality do you like the most and the least?

Chapter 5

Knowing is Seeing

Old ways won't open new doors. Decide what you want and "know" it is possible and "will" happen. Take the steps that can be taken and maintain a sense of gratitude "knowing" it is on the way.

I have now repeated the details of who we are, who you truly are numerous times, and I'll continue to do so, intentionally, with the hope that it becomes an affirmation, where you absorb the details and come to really KNOW who you are. It takes consistent reminders to have it settle into a place of comfort in which it is an awareness present day-to-day, minute-to-minute. The goal is for self-realization of who you are to become a happiness trigger that creates a joy-filled life. It's so easy to have events, experiences, things heard and said color your thinking and reactions. These situations occur over and over, and each time they cover over—conceal—who you really are … God. These cause and effect, give and take, action and reaction events develop as habits and continue until you intervene and begin to change your own patterns.

I have come up with a ritual that I do dozens of times a day, some days more often than others. Throughout the day, I repeat a phrase I choose to be a trigger or a switch to draw or flip myself out of what I'm focused on or thinking about. Once I activate the switch, I instantly come to a place of being present or conscious of who I really am as God right now.

My phrase is "I Am," (I Am God), and it directs me away from my train of thought to being present, to remembering who I truly am. It's my way to remind myself that I am not all the "stuff" that is happening around me.

The phrase or switch can be anything that resonates with you. Examples of the word could be Flip, Blink, Now, Shift, or Spirit. Some people like the traditional sound of Shalom or Peace. It only matters that you choose a word or phrase that will draw you out of what is happening at the moment and into a place of comfort, security, and knowing that you are God. While you remain grounded in It, life and your energy will flow from perfection and love.

Belief comes from the mind, while knowing comes from the heart.

When you believe something with your mind you are saying, "I believe this is true, but it might not be." Your ego creates a space in case there is failure. Belief can then enter and call it its new home, leaving space for change. But when you say, "I KNOW it is true," then there is no space left. Your certainty fills the void, and you are telling God's Love that you have the authority to decide what is, and what isn't. You declare what you want, and it is created. Knowing is seeing.

Loving someone is a great example. Since you believe the person is a separate individual, forming a relationship creates a oneness that brings you joy. Love is the closest you as a human get to feeling what it is to be fully God, which is why love feels so complete and awesome. Love comes from the heart. It comes from knowing.

Your individual life-plan or goal is another example of God's desire and expression of individuality. If you had no individual personality, no opportunity for individual expression and to learn and grow would exist. You'd already have full knowing of who and all that you are. The personality brings a separation, a veil that allows God to experience life as each of us within a human body and experience life as an individual, we each learn and make one-of-a-kind choices. The personality is the gift of individuality.

I think back to my youngest memories and my thoughts as a young student in middle-school and high school, a young married woman, giving birth to children, being employed, experiencing family and friends, creating businesses, buying old cars and new cars, renting homes and then buying properties, and so on. What I see swings from one extreme of the spectrum to the other. Joy and love to self-bashing and absolute dread and hatred. Now knowing every thought creates, it is a surprise I survived.

Luckily, creative thoughts through your personality are, in a sense, diluted. You need layers of similar thoughts to bring about creation, which needs concentrated knowing. This is why repetition is important to create what you truly want.

Pause for just a moment and think back over your life. It is so easy to think back on all the negative thoughts, fears, dreads, and anxieties and see how they came about just as you expected. You were right, meaning you were a very successful creator.

This is interesting. When you were born, you only had two innate fears. You were afraid of falling and loud noises. That was it, you had no other fears. Everything else that you became afraid of was learned.

All your other fears fall into three categories: 1) not feeling worthy, 2) not feeling loved, 3) not feeling safe. Falling and loud noises fall into the not feeling safe category.

This is where the signal or switch, the "I Am" phrase is important and comes into play. You can use it whenever you remember to draw yourself away from life's craziness and back into being aware of who you truly are, where you intentionally focus on what you genuinely want in your life --what is important to you.

Points to Ponder

- Make it a practice and a goal to remind yourself that you are God and, on a path, to creating a joy-filled life.
- Create a way to switch to a state in which you affirm who you really are. Consider it your happiness tool. Use it when you are confused, in turmoil, or feeling negative about your life. I use "I am" as a mantra; you can use it, too, or find one that feels like a fit.
- Creation required layers of thought, which is why repetition is important in your practice.
- Understand that "believing" leaves room for doubt; knowing is complete and solid; no room to waver. Remind yourself as often as possible that *Knowing is Seeing.*

QUESTIONS TO CONSIDER

1. What rituals have you developed to nurture yourself?
2. What makes you feel loved? What makes you feel unloved?
3. What are rituals you can create for better self-care?

Chapter 6

Unconscious Practices

I feel it is super important for people to experience a joyful life. The best way to find "joy", which you'll discover is just as true for finding success or money, is to focus less on the "results" of a life well lived and more on the life well lived. Stay in the moment. Experience joy now. Simple is as simple does.

It was later in life that I implemented this mental tool, but I also recognize that in less formal ways, I've been unknowingly using a directed focus for much of my life.

For about four years in the early 1980s, Jack and I attended a church called the Universal Church of Ontology. Wikipedia says: Ontology is a branch of philosophy that studies concepts such as existence, being, becoming, and reality. It includes the questions of how entities are grouped into basic categories and which of these exist on the most fundamental levels. This definition sounds a lot like what we have been discussing.

It was about this time that the church and its principal members, some of them "priests" (their word) of the church, decided something was brewing in the world, some major change was coming, and they were going to move to North Carolina, and, if other members wanted to join or follow the Church, they were welcome to come.

I don't recall all the reasons we decided to make the move and join the group, but that's what Jack and I did. In part, I'm sure we made the decision because we were friends with many members. Perhaps being bored with our routine life in Jacksonville nudged us to make a change. Jack had hurt his back and designing and installing lawn irrigation systems was trying for him. Plus, Jack's mother passed away that year and staying in town to be close to my mom and Abbott wasn't a priority.

We sold our house, and most all our possessions and moved to the country near Asheville, North Carolina. We shared a large house with other church members, but the plan was to build several other houses on the acreage of the property as a community.

This arrangement for us lasted about four or five months, but then it became all too much. Jack left the community first and got a job selling recreational vehicles (RVs) in Asheville. He set up a tent in a campground until he earned enough money to consider getting an apartment. He was a salesman at heart and with his experience selling furniture with Abbott, he quickly became their top salesman.

Aside from one other young girl, my kids were the only children in this adult group. Finally, the kids and I realized we were out of place, but that came before I found the strength needed to move away without the underpinning of a place to go, and furniture and regular household necessities. Eventually, though, we left the rural area, and Jack and I found a rental house in Asheville. The move to the mountains led the church itself to become disjointed. When it came to day-to-day living and the need for flexibility in this unique living situation, the church's teachings weren't so firmly embedded in the people who made the move. In other words, personalities changed.

Still, once in the rental house, I held Sunday teaching sessions for the kids in our living room. I wanted to instill the principles of living a spiritual life. My beliefs hadn't changed. I just didn't want to live that close to other people, and they didn't want to live that close to us and three kids.

Jack sold RVs, and I started wood-burning and painting decorative decoy ducks for a small craft company, who then sold the wooden ducks at craft shows around the mountains of North Carolina. In the afternoons, after Jack got home from work, he and I would drive through the mountains looking and dreaming about finding a piece of mountain land that we could call our own. We loved the mountains. Truly, they felt like we had come home after being away a long time. It was hard to explain, but there was an inner connection.

A year into our North Carolina adventure, our oldest daughter finished the eleventh grade and took some college classes during the summer. At that point, we decided we needed to move back to Jacksonville. She was a gifted student with the desire to go to a university, and that wasn't going to happen with the money we were making in North Carolina. We weren't able to buy a piece of mountain land, either, not with the money Jack earned selling RVs, or from what I was paid for each carved duck I produced.

One year after separating from the church group, we moved back to Jacksonville, but with the desire to earn the money needed to come back to North Carolina to live on our own piece of property.

We rented a house in Jacksonville. Jack went back to doing lawn irrigation systems, and I created soft-sculpture dolls and my own carved decoy ducks. On the weekends, Jack would set up a display at craft shows in the local malls and sell what I created during the week.

I drew a thermometer on a piece of craft paper and taped it

in the hallway of our house. With every hundred dollars we saved, I colored in a rising level. The goal was to earn the money needed for a down payment for a house in the mountains of North Carolina.

Later that year, Jack worked a craft show a couple weeks before Christmas, and a man came up to his display, looked at the decoy carvings and then glanced at our business card. He asked Jack why he called the company Carolina Collectables if his address was Jacksonville, Florida. Jack laughed and explained we used to live in Asheville, and we hoped to get back there.

The man told Jack he owned five acres in the mountains of North Carolina north of Asheville. Jack told him he knew the area well. We'd driven through it many afternoons as we dreamed of buying a piece of property in the country. The man gave Jack his phone number.

A couple days later, I called the man. I told him we were interested in his property, but we couldn't look at it until spring break, four months in the future, when the kids were out of school for a week. "No problem," he said. "I'm looking for the right buyer. I'm in no hurry."

As you can guess, in April that next year, we shook hands and bought the property on top of a mountain with views that look into Asheville 40 miles away. We still live there today, more than 35 years later. So, here is how I look at the series of events: Paradoxically, or so it seemed, we needed to follow our heart, our guidance, and leave the place we wanted to be. We had to do what needed to happen so our daughter could get a scholarship to follow her dream, while also earning the money we needed to creatively buy a piece of property in North Carolina. Without these steps, we wouldn't have our dream home. As it happened, the landowner of the property let us pay him directly. I wrote up the agreement, and we paid off the cost of the land in seven years, paying as we were able.

Our oldest daughter completed a successful senior year in Jacksonville and earned a scholarship to a prestigious university in Washington, DC. She graduated and has lived in numerous places and earned other college degrees along the way. She married and had two children and created the life she envisioned for herself.

Jumping ahead into more recent history, my daughter and her husband moved to North Carolina in 2019, eight months before the start of the Covid19 epidemic. She and her husband wanted to live closer to Jack and me, but she also wanted to work, and she's both a librarian and a teacher. She accepted a position teaching in Asheville. In January 2020, a month before Covid19 was identified and after teaching just four months, she got a call out of the blue about one of the positions she had applied for nearly a year before. Of all the jobs she's applied for, it had been the one she wanted most. So, she took the leap, accepted a position as the Director of the County Library System in the county where we all live.

It was all an incredible sense of timing. One month into a new job that she was just learning, Covid struck, and businesses everywhere began closing. Instead of closing completely, my daughter devised a plan to provide curbside and virtual services to help residents who were all now homebound. During the entire period of Covid, her libraries never closed. In our rural area, being innovative about maintaining access to books and other services was a top priority. The system she managed was one of a very few in the entire state to never close during that period. This may not have been the case if she hadn't been willing to leave a secure job and take the risk to accept the new position she'd wanted so badly.

So, although I've skipped around a bit, the point in these two examples is that "knowing" what we want and working toward it, brings it into reality even if in the most unexpected ways. Jack and I first moved to the mountains and into a situation that didn't work as expected, but then we made a new way in this special place we loved. We made a decision to leave it behind in order to find a way to get back permanently to our special place. Stretching even further, that knowing, and achievement brought about events that benefited not only us as a family, but thousands of other people 35 years later when my daughter and her family returned to the area.

Without a doubt, I have come to understand and know that when we are aware and make our desires known, God's energy as us pulls the pieces into place. With intention, I drew a paper money thermometer and passed it every day in the hall, "knowing" it was going to happen. And so, it did, but I couldn't have orchestrated the positive way our plan fell into place.

Now I intentionally use my "I Am" switch to zero in on drawing myself out of hectic daily routines and into a state of being present so I focus on what I truly want in my life.

QUESTIONS TO CONSIDER

1. What are some habits you unconsciously practice?
2. How do these habits influent you or impact your thinking?
3. Do you think unconscious habits can be healthy and beneficial?

Chapter 7

Thoughts Create Your Reality

Your thoughts and beliefs are the creators.

Depending on your mindset and objective, you can view your individual personality and your desires as a gift or a curse. If you believe life happens "to" you and you have no power to create what happens, you're apt to dread it rather than bless it.

You may often have one thought, and with the next thought, you change our mind. Understanding that each thought creates, it's no wonder that for much of your life you believe you're surrounded by a cloud of negativity, or, at other times, you experience life as haphazard, shifting moment-to-moment, week-to-week.

Pause for a second to analyze your thoughts, or at least most of them. Thoughts create your reality. Speaking adds even more strength. Consider how often throughout the day you think or say, I want this. I desire that. I hate this. I need this. I'm dreaming of this. I believe this will happen sometime. I believe I will have or get this. I must have this, or I have to do this to get that.

Think about what you are creating with these thoughts. Want, desire, hate, need, dreams, and believing something will be, and you must have this or that, or what you have to do to get this or that. Over and over, through what you think and what you say you create a mix of wants, needs, beliefs, and on and on.

So, thoughts and words create want and need, which then leads you to dream, compare, and change your mind. Then you want something else. This is how you create "want" in your life over and over again.

Instead, you benefit greatly if you create the reality you desire through thoughts and speaking as if it is already a reality. This means making an intentional change, so you think and say with conviction: I have this. I am this. I love my this or that. Or I like this. You get the picture…I know I am this or I have this. I am grateful for this or that. Knowing adds a deep connection and enhances emphasis, so you are linked to the reality of its actual existence and eventual appearance or happening.

As you move through this understanding, the goal is that you experience the lasting all-encompassing joy that is already within you, to realize and experience love, joy, abundance, and the effortless life you deserve.

Rather than God being something outside of yourself that you reach up to or search for to draw down into your mind, you come to understand that God is who you already are. It is ALL you are. It is already within your body. It waits to be discovered, revealed, recognized, and allowed to cast Its influencing light over your physical life, thoughts, reactions and emotions.

I'm suggesting It is All there is. It is everything or is in everything or makes up everything seen and unseen. Again, It is All there is.

I'd like you to say, "God." Having said it, I am truly suggesting that you and I are God.

Now, this might still seem far-fetched, so let's slow down and pick this apart so you fully grasp what's being revealed and shared. You can incorporate this divine concept into your life and perhaps also figure out how to bring love, joy, and abundance in all its forms into your experience. So, let's simplify the topic and put it in terms that are easy to understand.

Imagine a chocolate tasting event. LOL I love chocolate. I have one small piece most evenings. Yet, to look in my cupboard you would think I was hoarder. This love of chocolate probably goes back to those Heath bars Mom doled out as a reward for a good foot rub.

Okay, so let's have a chocolate party.

At a chocolate tasting, that's what it's all about—tasting.

Of course, there is conversation, too, because with chocolate there is plenty to learn and talk about. Depth of flavor, sweetness, bitterness, expectations, savoring, dislike, joy… There's no end to what can be said about chocolate. Yet, if all your learned or perceived ideas were discussed, that wouldn't begin to approach the taste of a single sliver of chocolate.

It's the same with God. But, for the moment, let's still keep this more personal and about life, yours and mine.

Your life has many aspects, including—your physical form, past experiences, families, goals or objectives, your future, your thoughts and emotions, employment/business/avocation, your beliefs and fears, expectations and regrets, dreads and satisfaction, happiness, appreciation, joy, hurt, your loves, longings, pain, dislikes, and loathing. The list could go on, and so many things in your life fit into many of these "categories." But what is most important is what you know with certainty.

What you learn or know about God may be delightful or unsettling. However, what you know, understand or have experienced is apt to feel as if you're standing on the outside looking in. God and your knowledge of It is once removed, merely an inkling, rather than actual Life with a capital "L" or God within

Life, or more importantly, within your life. It's as if you're anticipating or imagining the taste without savoring it.

And then, if or when, you do experience a brief encounter with God, you savor a sliver of chocolate for a brief time. It's glorious, but just a taste that lacks the realization that you are the chocolate. You are the chocolate, and you are the taster, tasting life.

As I was writing this section, something cool happened. My daughter texted and asked if the next time I drove down the road past her house if I would bring her a couple Heath Bars from my cupboard. We are all one. It is right there and connects us if we develop a sensitivity to it and pay attention. Synchronicities like this feel like exclamation points!!!!

Points to Ponder

- When you think about God you are looking within to who you are—no need to draw God to you. It is already you and everything you see, hear, touch, taste, or smell, or imagine, is God, too.
- Notice your thought language: I want, I need, I wish…now direct your thoughts as if these desires are here, present tense, not was, not will be, but now.
- The life you want is within you; it is yours to reveal; unleash the joy that is God as you.

QUESTIONS TO CONSIDER

1. What are some negative results you are currently creating with your thoughts?
2. What are some new thoughts you could focus on to create positive results?
3. What actions can you practice to keep your thoughts positive instead of defaulting to negativity?

Chapter 8

Living an "Aware" Life

Stay aware that happiness isn't a destination. It's a knowing that things couldn't be any better than having the ability to perceive what you desire and to think what you choose. When you fully grasp this concept, it is magical.

So, besides merely reading this, you're invited to taste what it means to actually be Life, to be God, to live God's Life as "you". Or, put another way, you permit God to live through you, rather than just knowing information about God, which appears to exist "out there," or separate from you.

First of all to be God, or have God living through you, doesn't God have to be actually alive? Doesn't God have to be vital, living? God is nothing if not alive and here now.

Certainly, you can say, "I am alive, I am conscious right now. Right, this second!" By being quiet and still for a moment, you find you are experiencing a gentle feeling of simply being alive, or you have an awareness of being alive.

But what exactly is that? I'm not talking about thoughts that God is alive, but about the "alive stuff" Itself. It's the you that is alive and here right now prior to thoughts arising about it. At this level, God is only feel-able, alive-able—not think-able. It just is, or more correctly, you simply are God. This is the Spirit of God.

Pause for a second to experience this. You are God. It is within you. It may be covered over or buried beneath layers of louder stuff—your emotions and thoughts, fears, desires, past memories, worries or concerns, longings, love, pain, needs, and so on. It may be covered so well you're unaware of Its presence, but It is there.

Notice that when consciously putting attention on this feeling of inner God, it becomes a conscious awareness of God.

At the beginning of this book, it was stated that once you initiate awareness, your path can't help but bring you forward, paving the way for new experiences that open the door for growth. Awareness allows you to consciously evolve.

So, now you are aware of God.

When spiritual thought or consideration are somewhat new to you, the feeling of the alive presence of God may seem ethereal or faint at first—like a soft whisper. What obscures God is the tendency to focus on what cries out loudest and demands the most attention— sights, sounds, touches, thoughts, and emotions like those mentioned earlier. They demand attention while blocking everything else out with their sensory noise and urgent need for us to notice and pay attention to them.

So how do you become aware of God and let Its presence guide your life?

Imagine a TV blasting in a room so loudly you can't hear a soft whisper. The whisper is there, potentially perceptible, but it's covered over. Gently persist—without thinking—Shhh, It is there, consciously feel this gentle sense of God. Let Its subtle voice influence and guide you.

As you've noticed, if you want to speak to someone in a noisy, crowded room, you lean in close and whisper. You don't yell to be louder than the room's noise. If you try that, you'll strain your throat and add to the chaos in the room. Likewise, that still voice of God within you doesn't try to compete with the mental chatter on the surface of your mind, nor does it attempt to overpower the noise of the outside world. If you want to hear it, no matter what is going on around you or even inside you, you can always tune into that soft voice underneath the surrounding noise. This is your way to lean in close to focus only on that sound.

The more persistent voices in your head delivering messages that make you feel panicky or afraid have questionable validity. They may be voices you have internalized from childhood or from your family's beliefs or culture, and as such, they possess only half-truths. Their persistent urgency stems from their disconnectedness from the center of your being, your heart, the Spirit of God, but their pushiness is what catches your attention.

God's voice whispers reassurances that everything is okay and delivers its message with quiet confidence. Once you hear it, you know it speaks the truth. Often once you have heard what it has to say, a powerful sense of calm settles over you; the other voices and sounds, once so frantic and pushy, fade into the background and suddenly seem small and far away.

Once recognized and accepted, the quiet certainly of God may influence your thoughts and the words you speak in your everyday settings. As you become more interested in maintaining your connection to the whisper of truth, which shares its message like the sound of the wind rustling the leaves of a maple tree, you may be less inclined to take part in idle chatter. As you align yourself more with this quiet confident presence, you become an extension of the whisper. You slide through the noise of the world and create more peace, trust, and confidence with your own soft, wind-swept rustle. You change your thoughts and speech from you want, desire, hate, need, and must have, to thoughts and speech of knowing you have, you are, and you love.

"Tuning in" through conscious awareness leads you to clarity that this alive, aware presence is not something, you personally, are responsible for. You don't cause the Spirit of God to be present within you. Like the unheard whisper It has always been there. Yet now you are aware of God and can zero in on Its whispered words, which become louder as other attention-seeking distractions fall back and become quieter.

Neither you nor I, as a thinker, know how to think God into being alive. Does anyone know how to make consciousness be conscious? Of course not.

It is God Itself that is being aware.

Pause now and see if you can shut off conscious being-alive awareness, or make it go away. You can't because it is God Itself not "the personal you" that is being alive and aware.

Points to Ponder

- God is aliveness, so focus on life, knowing your thoughts create your life.
- Practice being in the stillness of God as you and you as God. Awareness may come in a soft whisper, like a gentle breeze, bringing you back to the awareness of creation.
- Notice how you feel when you switch your focus from what you don't like or don't want to the joy of creating through God's Love.

QUESTIONS TO CONSIDER

1. When and where do you feel most alive, most vital, most yourself?
2. What external distractions are making it hard to be aware and hear your own thoughts, feelings, needs, emotions?
3. What actions can you take to live a more "aware" life?

Chapter 9

Existence Within and In Spite of You

Oh, get excited now, because there are more potentials, more possibilities, more opportunities here for you than have ever existed before.

God's alive presence is not just an idea or theory, not a belief of an author named Wendy. Why? Theories and beliefs consist of thoughts. Your alive God is not something being thought—either by me or by you. It is purely God born and living as you. It has been there with you since before your first breath.

Today's young generation might easily be able to think of themselves and you as avatars. You live and experience life for a span of time, and then, when the game or episode is over, you wake up from the avatar's dream life. You resume the real God aspect of life until you choose to take on a new avatar to experience a new life as a human being. Your "real" Self is there within you all through this avatar experience. It is concealed within the outer appearance of the avatar.

If the term avatar is new to you, check Yourdictionary.-com's definition, which goes beyond the title of a movie. An avatar is something visual used to represent non-visual concepts or ideas, or is an image used to represent a person in the virtual world of the Internet and computers. An example of an avatar is an icon you use to represent you on an Internet forum.

Wikipedia says an avatar is a concept in Hinduism that means "descent" and is the material appearance or incarnation of a deity on earth. The related verb to "alight, to make one's appearance" is sometimes used to refer to any guru or revered human being.

Move from the word avatar to God. Just discussing the word God, the process involves thinking. So, it seems you are experiencing two things at once: 1) reading words and having thoughts about God, and 2) being the actual alive God Itself. Both involve you.

So, which are you, really?

You are conscious and alive. Words and thoughts are what you are conscious of. Words and thoughts by themselves are never conscious—only you are conscious. So, that's what you really are, pure consciousness or God, not unconscious words and thoughts about consciousness or about God. Huge difference: Thinking is a changing process. God is a changeless Divine Presence.

Experiencing yourself as God's conscious aliveness Itself, beyond just pondering it, yields many new insights.

For a moment, say the word "I" silently. Don't say it aloud. Let "I" be said silently within.

Repeat "I" (I am God) — slowly and softly—I, I, I, until you clearly hear I within yourself. That which is saying I is like an "inner voice," and it's invisible. This invisible voice obviously is not the same as a visible object, such as your body.

Let me share the key—don't first identify yourself as the visible body and assume "it" is the one now saying I. Start to identify directly as God, zero in on this invisible voice only. Deal only in terms of God.

A physical mouth or vocal cords are not saying "I," are they? It's clear that "I" is being said, but isn't heard by physical ears, is it? Fingers can't touch I. Nor can I be tasted or smelled. I has nothing to do with the five physical senses.

God as the invisible I, by Itself, is not a physical object with a form. Awareness is invisibleness only. So, when you say, "I am alive and conscious," You cannot be referring to your body because your visible body is not the aliveness of the invisible I or God.

Then, where does your invisible voice "come from"? It arises out of pure conscious God, which is invisible.

Note your conscious awareness of the voice, but it's not the same as God. The very voicing of I is still a kind of mental form. The conscious alive God that gives rise to I is completely formless.

Conscious alive God, in terms of Itself alone, also has no solidity. If you could poke a finger into God, you wouldn't feel any substance or density.

What about heaviness or weight? If anything, pure God seems to consist of incredible softness and lightness. Take a moment to really notice, feel, this unspeakable lightness. It truly is a nothingness.

In the same way, God has no physicality or length, width or height or weight. No dimensions, but it is conscious, alive, and pure.

If you were to ask, "What is I made of?" this voice speaking within you seems similar to a thought. It seems to come and go. It's temporary. It arises from pure God consciousness, then dissolves back into it.

What remains in the silence when God is not speaking?

There is silence, stillness, what might be thought of as an

emptiness, but it isn't a void. It's full of the invisibility of an all-encompassing Love, but let's not go there just yet. The silence of God is unlimited and ripe for the unexpectedness of what is to come next.

The void is definitely not deadness or nothingness because the identity of "you" remains, very much alive and aware. You are the conscious creator of your life. God gives you the freedom of choosing your own course. You make the decisions. God gives you free choice. You decide what controls you; you choose what you want or desire and what you will give power to, and this happens through God's Love as you use Its power to create through thought.

Knowing is Seeing. Thoughts create. Concentrated, unwavering thoughts create more quickly. God creates through thought. Being aware of God and that It is who you really are adds power and certainty to your creativity.

Points to Ponder

- Consciousness is invisible, but awareness of It allows you the free choice embodied in the all-encompassing God.
- Yes, thoughts create, but directed, unwavering thoughts create more quickly and are a manifestation of "knowing is seeing."

Intentional Creation

Let's take a deep breath here. My head is buzzing. I am going to slow down and share how I use this new understanding and ability every day. Being aware that I am God, and that my thoughts create on a daily basis, I create. I don't flit from one thing to another. I decide what I want in my life, what I want to happen, and I focus a "knowing" on it.

With certainty, when I get into my car, I know my appointment or destination will be reached safely and will go well. I know I will find a front row parking place. If I merge into multilane traffic, I know there will be a half-block of empty road where I can merge easily across several lanes of traffic. I know I'll easily find what I'm looking for at the store. I know I'll always have the money needed to make my desired purchases. I know I'll easily and confidently share the needed information at an event. I know what I have to share will help others succeed in achieving abundance through option trading if that is what they desire and know for themselves. I know the projects I've created like building rental treehouses are going to go smoothly or be lined up in the best interest of the project. I know other people will love them. I know the time I have to devote to achieving my goals will be just the right amount of time. I know my small cabin home on top of a mountain with a breathtaking view is my safe place. I know I'll always love the people in my life no matter what personal choices they make.

My knowing, my true belief creates everything I want because my knowing is unwavering, and God, "me," creates.

Within God, there is a clean, inner quiet, a pure stillness—a wide open emptiness or spaciousness that is silently alive and aware that love is all there is. Love is God expressing Itself as you, and everyone and everything in all Its forms. This proves you are something far beyond who you believe yourself to be because even when "I" seems absent, you are present and alive with the ability to choose what you want filling and governing your life through your creative thoughts.

Not only is your alive God without physical limits, but pure God also Itself has no mental limits or conditioning either.

God is actual life itself, the real you. All the powers or abilities or creativeness within God are within you.

At any and every moment, it's possible to live a completely brand-new life. You are in charge and make the choices. You are in control of your emotional, mental, and physical decisions. You are in charge of your openness to allow God to shine Its love through you, giving you the creativeness available through God's Love. You create through your attention, thoughts, and desires.

Divine Life

Don't simply assume you are limited to a visible, weighty, 3-dimensional body. Not so!

Let yourself experience your actual divine life—as weightless, borderless, infinitely alive God every single second of every day.

What it really means to be living a divine life as you is to be alive as the invisible One Infinite Creator or God with unlimited powers.

Think about this for a moment, as pure invisible God, you are absolutely flawless! As this lightness of pure God, you are forever without baggage—none—not physical, mental, or emotional.

I. Am. Here. Now. Four synonyms for God. "I am here now" is also your autobiography.

It's not necessary to hold onto this effortlessly alive God. Because It simply can't and won't go away. It never leaves because It is life itself. Assume that you were previously unaware of Its presence and felt that the divine was some ethereal guiding force outside of you and the world as you knew it. Now accept that this God is present within you.

Again, for a moment, allow yourself to feel how un-dense and un-tense, how gently soft and light, your invisible alive God presence is. I say presence because that's where It is, within you, and everyone and everything. It's there or here. It's who you are whether you like it or believe it or not. You are God expressing Itself as the you, you choose to be. You are free to create the life you want through God's Love without limitations or restrictions.

So, you choose to become more aware of God and want Its guidance. Then now that you are aware, you'll benefit from a routine of spending a few moments being silently alive as pure, gentle conscious God. This quiet time spent in awareness of God is worth more than a month spent verbally trying to describe it.

Each time you zero in on this God awareness, you'll notice how there is no end to your softness-with-no-ceiling-or-floor. Everything consists of weightless ease.

Your life is a perpetual fountain of gentle alive peaceful flowing light that never runs dry. Love freely flows through you. Situations that may once have been a bother melt away. Relax and enjoy yourself in your exquisite, never runs out God that shines Its flowing light and glow on every aspect of your life.

This is life's meaning—to forever be alive as the never-ending God, of us, of you, and me!

This is true regardless of awareness, that is, whether anyone and everyone you know or see are aware of God or not. It is there within them, and It is allowing them to create the life they desire or the elements of life they choose to focus on. It is freewill. Everyone you see at the grocery store, the car repair shop, running a cash register, driving a school bus, waiting tables in a restaurant, stacking shelves at the department store, and working in an office is God.

It's interesting that people who manifest peace by being aware of God are not different from you; they have chattering thoughts and troubled emotions just like you do. The difference is that they do not extend or place their energy on those thoughts and feelings. Instead, they're aware that these feelings come and go, rising and falling like the waves the ocean, but without disturbing the deeper waters of peacefulness and love residing at their core.

You can also have a hidden fear of becoming aware of God or moving into Its light of love. You fear Its light will expose areas of darkness within your personality. You fear exposure or perhaps, releasing the beast, the ugliness.

Points to Ponder

- Life is all there is, and you are life experiencing a body now, with free will to create your unfolding life.
- Go about your day knowing you are more than your body and your random undirected thoughts. Experience what it feels like to know your day is your perfect expression of God's Love as you.
- Note changes in your moods, emotions, evaluations, expressions when you remember who you really are.
- If you find yourself caught up in a stream of negative thoughts or you are caught up in negativity about the past or you dread something ahead of you, try repeating to yourself: *I am here now…I am here now…I am here now.*

An Internalized Practice

You have the ability to choose to spend your energy on these negative tendencies of personality created by indecision and conflict. Since you have a choice about how to spend energy, practice enables you to grow increasingly confident and more serene as you choose the positive energy of God. You begin to see your thoughts and feelings as tiny specks floating on the surface of your life. They pose no threat to the deep interior stillness and centeredness of God that is the light and source of your personal peace.

You can look out over everyone you encounter and know they, too, are God. They are not better, more fortunate, or less or more broken or hopeless. They are God experiencing life at a chosen, self-designed or at a selected point that is right for them until, based on their life experiences and personality, it no longer serves their greater good. They also have a life goal or objectives that they can choose to follow or ignore.

Often when I am at the grocery store, I will take a few minutes to lean back against the meat counter and observe others in the store. Watching a mother and her children over by the milk and juice section, reminding myself that each of them is God, and they are creating their lives based on their thoughts, beliefs, and choices. The elderly couple, who each cling to the cart for support, have created their lives and have had the opportunity to influence others through their thoughts, desires, and actions. The middle-aged man who comes in and selects a bouquet of flowers, along with a bag of potatoes. Maybe wife asked him to pick them up on his way home. The guy behind the meat counter packaging ground meat is showing a young employee how to cover and seal it with clear wrap. Each of them is experiencing the same action, but likely will take away something different. We are all God, individual parts of the same whole.

After this moment of appreciative observation, I try to greet everyone I pass with a sincere expression of love, recognizing who they really are. By doing so, I am loving myself in a dozen different forms.

As a child in the process of growing and developing your personality, much of the connection to nature and to the Universe is removed from your human experience. So much so, you tend to forget that you are a product of the natural world. At the moment of birth, you are perfectly attuned to nature. Your feelings are an authentic response to every stimulus you encounter. You interact with your personal, physical world through your senses, wanting only what is necessary for your survival. As years pass, however, you discover the sights, sounds, scents, and stimulation of the outside world. Though this stimulation momentarily dazzles you with glitz and excitement, the inner, sometimes, seemingly cloudy memory of who or what you really are remains. It doesn't disappear, but God gets covered over by your personality as it strengthens and imbeds itself in the glitter of the outside world.

If or when you embrace the idea that human beings are inherently natural elements of God, you can bring It to the forefront of your day-to-day experience. This allows you to achieve a new level of wellness that boosts and strengthens the creative power that resides at your very core. You become active, intentional creator rather than casual participant.

This brings us back to why Spirit of God would desire to experience life as an individual or more correctly nearly eight billion people. Consider the varied experiences, likes, dislikes, education, and cultures where each is unique and has the ability to create anything that comes to mind, and all are willing to work to bring it into physical reality.

An Analogy

Not long ago, I had a discussion with a man who to some degree agreed with the concept of God, God's Love, and the Spirit of God. He stressed his belief, but he still found it hard to incorporate the overall concept to the point it settled into a comfortable place of understanding for him. In other words, he hadn't fully integrated the belief within his everyday life.

"I know, it is all ethereal, nothing you can see or touch," he said, "but isn't there some physical example that would help me better grasp all this?"

I suggested that he—you—imagine that God is an Ocean, an invisible Ocean. The Ocean is everywhere and a part of It or the essence of It is everywhere and is in everything. The Ocean's invisible presence is incorporated into every rock, tree, soil, sky, planet, solar system, manmade item, animal, and person.

Now, imagine that periodically a Drop of the Ocean pops up out of the Ocean somewhere, but, of course, It is still connected to the invisible Ocean. But for that moment, It seems separate and is able to forge Its own way. The Drop comes down to earth, slips into a body to become an embryo and is born. It then begins Its life as a human being. This new human doesn't realize that within the body what It really has (and is) is a Drop of the invisible Ocean.

As the Drop's human body ages, and life plays out in its physical form, all that It experiences colors who the Drop is. Emotions, feelings, perceptions, experiences, understanding, and knowledge are absorbed and become part of the Drop, which means those insights becomes part of the invisible Ocean as well. It doesn't change the Ocean, and yet all that is added through the life experience is instantly accepted as it happens and is shared throughout the whole of the invisible Ocean.

The Drop, as a human, experiences life and depending on its goals and personal circumstances and drive, it may never become aware of the internal invisible Ocean at its core or base of who it is. Should physical death of the body take place, the body decays, but the Drop of Ocean goes right back to being incorporated within the whole where Its life experiences have added color and zest to the whole Ocean. Every gram of the Ocean holds the life experiences of the Drop as well as the experiences of every other Drop that has lived a life.

At some point, the Drop may pop up to be born again. It's

still connected and is a part of the invisible Ocean, and, again, all that It experiences adds Its slight color to the Ocean as a whole. Perhaps, during this life experience, the human begins to ponder spiritual subjects, questions, and wants to understand what is at the core of life. What is it all about?

In this life, it stretches and comes to discover and understand that it's a part of something greater. It's a part of the Ocean, and it works on being aware of the Ocean and that awareness brings peace, joy, stability, and love to its life. This awareness brings with it an understanding that the Ocean that's within It at the core of Its life is also at the center of everyone else's life. Everyone and everything is connected and is part of the same all-encompassing Ocean. The gift and use of God's Love allows for an active awakening that initiates Its ability to consciously create.

This understanding also brings about a desire to observe, accept and put judgment aside and to love everyone because now you know you are all part of the same Whole, the Ocean.

You love yourself in a million or perhaps, billion different forms.

Points to Ponder

- To bring you to awareness of who you are, spend time observing everything in your world from a place of knowing it is all one in God, as God, and therefore, one with you.
- Consider God as an Ocean and you as a Drop and the person next to you as a Drop and almost eight billion other human beings on the planet as that many drops. Does this shift your internal awareness of God as all there is?

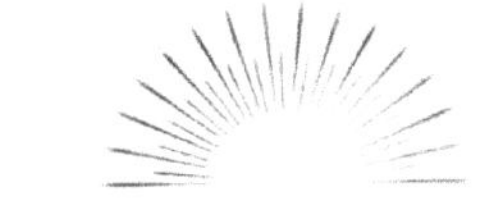

QUESTIONS TO CONSIDER

1. Have you stopped to consider the power you have to intentionally create and define your existence and the life you live?
2. Life exists beyond the boundaries of our bodies. What elements of divine life are missing from your existence?
3. What potential exists when you open your mind to the possibilities of life existing in different planes or consciousnesses?

Chapter 10

Force of Love

This might sound odd, but do you realize that whenever you feel love, for any reason what-so-ever, for trading, for a sunset, for an equity, for a piece of cake, for a trade pattern, for a child, or whatever, you irrevocably lift the entire world.

Love has been written about by the greatest philosophers, thinkers, and saviors in the world. The Love they spoke about, however, is very different from what most of us think and understand love to be.

The force of Love, with a capital L, is much more than loving your family and friends or loving a favorite food or model car because Love is not just an emotion. Love is a force. As a matter of fact, it is the strongest, most important and influential force in the Universe. In the grandest degree, it is the Universe.

It and Its expression of Itself is in all things. It is God expressing Itself through God's Love.

Love isn't weak or feeble. Love is the positive force of life. Love expressing Itself is the Creator and the cause of everything positive and good. It is also the gift of freewill expressing Itself as everything else.

You don't exist within a multitude of forces in life that create or hold things together. One is all there is.

The great powers of nature you have been taught, such as gravity, weak or strong nuclear interaction, electromagnetism, and so forth are invisible to you, but their power is indisputable. So, too, the force of Love as God is invisible as well, but Its power is above and beyond that of nature because It created those concepts and principles through Its own creative thoughts.

Go back to the list of Basic Concepts I mentioned earlier—clockwise and counterclockwise, together or apart, bright or dark, heavy or light, long or short, wide or narrow. These were likely created before physical creation.

What you see, feel and experience in any form is God' Love expressing Itself in a different, greater or lesser, degree.

Its Own Trinity

I want and hope you are beginning to understand that God and Its creative force of God's Love, the expression or act of loving is the same thing or varying degrees of the same thing.

As mentioned earlier, I've divided the concept of God into three segments: The "Force" of Love is God, and the "Act" of Loving, expressing Love or creating is God's Love. The third segment is the "Spirit" of God. (God, God's Love, and Spirit of God, which is each of us, is a personal expression of God.)

God is everything, in everything. It is the creator creating through thought as the expression of God's Love. It is expressing Itself out of or through Itself. There is nothing or nowhere It is not.

That said, this means you have been created by God out of Love. You are a part of Love and made from and out of Love.

You are God expressing Love as you. When you love your child or friend or dog or chocolate, you are God or Love expressing love.

God expressing and creating through God's Love is the Creator of All Things, expressing Itself, Its Spirit as you, and when you express love, you are God expressing love in whatever way or direction you choose and through that expression, you are creating.

The truth for all eternity and, more specifically, all your life, has been hidden in plain sight.

The reason the truth of who you are has been elusive throughout your life and throughout much of history rests in the limited concept you have been taught. The limitation leads to the belief that you are your body and mind.

You came into this world in a body with a mind you learn to use to discover that you are not the body and the mind. It sounds like a riddle. It certainly seems paradoxical until you absorb what it means.

You are God living life as you. If this God is all there is, then It is everything and is in you. This means you are a creator. You get to choose what you want in your life.

What you think, say, and do is a choice: You tell God's Love, the creative act of Love, what you want and desire in your life. Knowing is the power. Knowing is Seeing!

The reality of God's Love is so close you can't see it, and it's so subtle your mind can't grasp its power. This creative expression is so simple it's hard to accept the truth of it.

When you fully realize the truth, you then know you are enough. You're good enough. You're great enough. You're resourceful enough to be great and to be anything you choose to be. Or to have anything you choose to have.

Points to Ponder

- God's Love is a force; It "powers" the actions of all that is.
- When God—and you—create anything, you're expressing God's Love.
- The third part of this Trinity, the "Spirit" of God, is you—all of us, really—each an expression of God.
- The Oneness means that you can't be separated from God, God's Love, or the Spirit of God that you are.

QUESTIONS TO CONSIDER

1. Have you experienced the power of love? What was that experience like?
2. What would it be like to include yourself in love's all-encompassing power – not just your own love force but the force of everyone around you?
3. What is a goal you dream of accomplishing with the power of love?

Chapter 11

Life Through a Different Lens

When various points of view are compared, in the final analysis, the most important thing is not always who is right or wrong, winner or loser… but who put forth the greatest effort in considering the other perspectives by taking in the whole picture. There is a lot to learn and lots to share.

Despite this new or growing understanding, you can still become consumed and disturbed by life events created up to this point. What about all the hardships, negative issues and problems, disappointments, pain and suffering you have experienced?

Consider this. You go to a movie about war and conflict, courage and camaraderie and, after leaving the theatre, you say, "Geez, what a wonderful movie." You took in its totality. Your life is a cosmic picture show. It is exactly the same. It has ups and downs, disappointments, accomplishments, and victories. Taken as a whole, it is a masterpiece. Memorable, original and one-of-a-kind.

Earlier, I mentioned personal life events of physical and sexual abuse, cruelty, experiencing lack of love and abandonment, struggles, and hurtful comments. These things occurred, but all those events, good and bad, created me and who I am now. I wouldn't want to change any of those events to be someone else. I truly like who I am and that means all of those previous events served a meaningful purpose.

I once read a children's book called *Little Soul and the Sun: A Children's Parable* by Neale Donald Walsch, author of *Conversations with God*, to one of my grandchildren. In the story, there was a young angel who wanted to come to Earth to experience forgiveness. He begged, truly wanting an experience that would help him to gain strength and allow him to grow. Finally, another angel stepped forward and said he would come to Earth to be born, too, so he could create a set of circumstances that would give the young angel the opportunity to find and express forgiveness. He also hoped that the young angel would remember that performing this act that would need forgiving was a gift the young angel had requested.

Truly, it's no different for you. Each life event is a gift and gives you the opportunity to experience it and to grow.

When we first bought the property in North Carolina, Jack traveled to craft shows and sold the ducks we carved, and I woodburned and painted at home. He drove a day or two to the show location, did the show, drove back and then carved at home until he went to the next show. One day we attended a show in Asheville near the Biltmore Estate, which is a place where thousands of tourists come to visit each year. We instantly knew this area is where we should open a gift shop.

Pulling together nickels and dimes, we rented a small shop at the back of Biltmore Village, an area opposite the entrance to the famous Biltmore Estate. Over the course of the next five years, we upgraded our location two times until we located our shop in a historic home in the center of this tourist-visiting area. Jack worked the shop and carved where visitors could see him. It became a wonderful business where he no longer needed to travel and be away from home for days at a time. It also allowed us to buy a second home in Asheville, so we had the choice of staying close during the work week or driving the 45 miles to the mountain house. This was a small house our middle daughter had purchased and decided to sell because she and her husband wanted to move to Florida.

By becoming aware of God, you come to realize your life is like the movie as it is playing out. And no matter what happens, when it ends, it will be a great picture show with the best actors, cast and crew, scenery, sets, and a terrific director.

Being aware of God doesn't instantly dissolve everything disturbing or negative within your life. Those elements are apt to still arise now and again. They have been formulating for a while, and it takes time for them to dissolve. They once may have been all consuming and have dictated your emotions, reactions, and what you believed the future would bring based on the event. Yet, maybe, the complete opposite takes place.

Here is a perfect example. Jack and I had the gift shop in Asheville for twenty years where we sold wildlife carvings, and I sold my artwork, the work of other artists, and gifts. It was our one-and-only source of income as we raised our family and the kids attended college and then moved on with their lives. In 2004, there was a freak flood in the area of our shop, brought on by an unusual set of events, including heavy rains over a couple days, a river accidentally being dammed up by fallen trees, and a break in a reservoir. These events caused our shop and others in the area to flood with six feet of water. We had no flood insurance. It doesn't flood in the mountains of North Carolina.

It wiped us out. When the shop was open, we survived week to week through sales, juggling bill payments and expenses for our modest homes, health insurance, and school tuition for our youngest. The shop was going to be closed for months as it dried out, was cleaned up, floors and carpet torn out and replaced, and the inside reconstructed. Truly, we were in a desperate spot and had no idea how we were going to survive this set back.

A week or so after the flood a friend invited me to lunch as a pick-me-up and mentioned she had taken a couple weekly classes to learn to trade options on the stock market. I didn't have a clue what she was talking about, but I took the funds that had been set aside for the electric bill (the electric was off anyway) and signed up for the classes.

This new understanding of the stock market was a good fit for me. I won some trades, lost some, but realized I had a knack for trading. I studied on my own and, being an artist, I saw chart patterns in a different way than formally trained traders. Suddenly, I was earning more money than we ever made in the gift store. We had the funds needed to make the shop repairs, stock the shelves, and reopen.

Within two years or so, I wrote my first book to teach other women to trade options from home in their spare time. If it hadn't been for a devastating, freak flood that wiped us out, I would never have ever learned to trade options. At the time of the flood, I'd never even heard of options, despite the fact my father was an economics professor who taught students about the stock market.

The flood was an incredible gift, an unbelievable blessing in disguise. I now approach what might be seen as a negative event differently. I've learned to wonder what positive surprise the initial negativity will reveal. I am open for the possibility of it being a marvelous gift or opportunity.

Today, as something negative begins to take place, I find it wise to sit back, observe and be aware of the situation, but without adding any energy to it. I focus on being in the present moment. I've realized when I am present, I'm not thinking, I am just aware. Let the event or circumstance slowly move on and dissolve. Instead of trying to push the situation away or choosing to run away from it, which might be the normal reaction, welcome the situation and its eventual release, allow it to take place, while remaining aware that it's temporary and has no power.

When something that seems negative happens, don't connect with it. It is outside of you. Don't add energy or solidify it. You don't even need to try to understand it. Whatever is happening are just thoughts, feelings, and emotions being expressed about the situation, but they aren't you. Don't deny them or fight them. Just let them float on past without adding anything to them. By being and staying present, your view expands. You observe but aren't attached or affected by it. The situation dissolves and isn't internalized. Once you internalize a situation, it needs to be re-experienced over and over.

Points to Ponder

- Your life story may include cruelty or tragedy or many unpleasant experiences. You need not deny them, but you can acknowledge that they contributed to who you are.
- You have a choice to live in the negativity of the past or let it go. You can also express gratitude for the strengths you gained from the experience despite the pain.
- Take time to trace how one experience led to another created experience. Did a loss lead to a gain; did a hardship open a different door to opportunity?
- Knowing is Seeing isn't about "pretending" painful experiences didn't happen; it's about knowing that

you are not your experiences. You are God creating through God's Love.

- If negative thoughts about painful experiences or hurtful people intrude, you let them float on by. Direct your thoughts to what you want to create in your life.

Expanding Awareness

When in the present moment, your view or perspective seems to expand. It takes in the whole setting, everything in sight rather than specifics. In the present, you are an observer.

As you remain in the present moment, feelings and emotions soon pass and move away from you, leaving you with a peaceful feeling that you soon recognize as joy. This approach often reveals something new, a fresh opportunity, a revision or some positivity that wouldn't have been seen or realized without the "supposedly" negative experience.

As you practice this approach, you will prove to yourself that you are not your thoughts, feelings, or emotions. You are the one observing them. You will then be able to welcome emotions and situations as they arise and let them play out and fade away, so your life is no longer affected by rehashing and imagining all the what-ifs. You have become free because no matter what happens you are now an observer rather than a participant.

As you now know, I live in the mountains of Western North Carolina in a cabin near the top of the mountain. Not long ago, I was doing some crafting in the bright red barn at the base of the mountain, and I realized this special place was a clear analogy of what I have been experiencing on this spiritual journey of growth and accepting and actively incorporating God into my life.

At the barn throughout the day, a few cars pass, the mailman drives by and places envelopes and magazines in the boxes, neighbors' houses can be seen from two sides of the barn, rabbits, squirrels, deer and periodically, a groundhog or raccoon pass by. Over the years, two bears have visited. Any noise, the crush of gravel or a distant voice draws attention away from the task at hand because when I am in the barn, I am shut off and can't see what is happening outside the barn or in the surrounding woods. There can be a sense of uneasiness, not fear, but a level of apprehension because sight is limited since I can't see beyond the boundaries of being inside the barn. When I go outside, my sight is still limited to one side of the barn or the other because of its size. I can't see beyond the boundaries of what is known and visible.

Long ago, I realized that once you recognize and acknowledge your discomfort, you can then overcome it. It's impossible to overcome insecurities if you don't know what they are or where they come from. Fear is only frightening when you don't understand what you are afraid of. When you look at the cause of your concerns, the worries become known and are reduced to a manageable size. You can then study them and ask if they are reasonable. Once recognized, worry can be tackled with real, everyday solutions. By acknowledging your concerns, you gain the ability to release, erase, or ignore them.

Mountains can capture your imagination, summoning you to scale their heights, to circle in amazement at their feet and offer reverence at their greatness.

Mountains can be viewed for hundreds of miles away and if you are lucky enough to be on top of one, you can view other mountains, valleys, rivers, and the surrounding earth. Often mountains symbolize vision, and the ability to rise above the valleys and to view beyond your current location. From the top, you are able to witness life from a new perspective, to view your life in a new way. Towns that seemed large when you were in them appear tiny. You can take in the whole view in a single glance, which helps you put in perspective how large the world really is.

Mountains are almost always considered to be spiritual or holy places, and the energy at the top of a mountain is without a doubt special and unique. When you are at the top of a mountain, it is as if you have ascended into a purer space. The energy is lighter, yet more energized. Many people climb to the top of a mountain to connect with a higher source of growth and understanding, and many come back down feeling energized, stronger and wiser. Whenever you are feeling trapped or limited, a trip to the nearest mountain may be the cure you need.

There's a reason mountain views are so prized and special. It is because, even from a distance, mountains bring to mind how small you are, which often comes as a marvelous relief. They often illustrate your talent to connect with higher energy or spiritual source. Mountains rise from the earth, sometimes disappearing in foggy clouds that gather around and between them, as a symbol of the earth extending up into the heavens.

Let's say one day you come to visit me and choose to expand and move beyond what is known to you at and inside the barn. You decide to stretch beyond what you are comfortable with, and you head up the steep, windy gravel road running up the mountain. Up and around the first bend, you now see a portion of the valley and look down at the barn. The neighbors' houses are now in clear view, one on each side of the barn. You glance behind you and notice the steep road coming up to where you stand, and you realize there's nothing scary about the barn and surrounding area. Everything existing there serves a purpose. The fields produce hay. The pond provides fish and water for animals. The lonesome bay of a cow is saying it misses its calf that has moved to a different portion of the pasture.

You go up farther still, and perhaps new, unseen territory is an unknown, so maybe it's still a little scary. The windy road is super steep, but your view has opened even more, so you see sights that were once hidden. Mountain ranges, pastures, pines, oaks, maples, a creek, a large rock protruding out of a gentle slope—familiar sights after all. Your fear of the unknown is diminishing.

When you finally reach the top, you can see in all directions. Nothing is hidden from you. You can see expansive valleys, other mountains, sky and clouds slowly sliding past. You can see fog settling into the crevices between mountains farther away, and nearer the barn, fences, and neighbors' homes are farther away but in full view. You can see from where you are that you have nothing to fear from the valley or the winding road that brought you to the top, where the sheer beauty all around you is breathtaking.

You also become aware of how everything serves a purpose in its time and place. Everything is needed as if it is a stepping-stone that has taken you from one level of understanding to the next. You would not be who you are or have your current understanding or ability to apply this new awareness without having experienced and grown through all the levels of earlier happenings, positive and, often more important, negative.

You can also see other travelers at various stages on their way up the mountain and you realize the best part of being on top of the mountain was the trip up. The experiences, realizations and growth. From where you stand, there is expansiveness, infinite beauty and perfection. Nothing out of place, everything is exactly as it should be. The wonder of life, the limitlessness of creative inspiration is revealed to you. It's all there for you to enjoy. You can look up at the stars and sense the infinite, which is truly what you are and who you have always been—infinite God that creates through the power of God's Love. God is who you are, whether you are at the bottom of the mountain or at the top.

What You Create Comes from Yourself

Regularly remind yourself that you are an active creator, who continually draws everything into your life, depending on your thoughts, expectations, drive, goals, and emotions. Also remind yourself that divine Love's creative ability doesn't know negative words like "don't" or "hate." All it understands is your focused attention, your current knowing.

So, imagine what happens when you say or think over and over, I don't want to fail. I don't want to be broke all the time. I don't want to be late. I don't want to miss my flight. I don't want to mess this up. I hate mean people. I despise disrespect. I hate it when my car doesn't run well. I loathe feeling rushed. I hate it when I can't afford what I want to buy. I hate it when the store doesn't have what I need. I despise it when people disappoint me. I hate negativity.

There is nothing wrong with your mind. Your mind is a tool, and it runs on automatic. The problem comes when it constantly tells you there is lack in your world—lack of money, lack of friends, lack of success, lack of health, lack of love, lack of support, lack of abilities or resourcefulness, and lack of resources (everything), so there isn't enough to go around.

The mind can be a troublemaker, a trickster. If you believe the mind, rather than being in charge of your thoughts, recognizing it as being creative, then what it brings up repeatedly, adding strength each time it comes to mind, is exactly what you'll experience. You then reinforce or add credibility to the thought being true. It becomes what you know. It is a vicious circle because Knowing is Seeing. Or put another way, if you have a list of things you don't want, you're likely to see many items on that list show up.

Again, the mind is a trickster. Interesting to note, there's no such thing as "when." When this happens, I'll get that. When I know this, I'll do that. The future is forever changing, and what changes "when" is "now."

Let's discuss a hypothetical story of being in charge of your thoughts. You can take the main role in this story. Let's say you have been working at a job for a while and, overall, you believe you've absorbed the initial training. In fact, you've begun to have a few creative ideas about ways to improve clients' experiences and overall customer service.

One day during lunch, you tell a couple of coworkers you have a great idea and wonder how you should go about sharing it with the department head. One of the co-workers says, "One time I shared an idea with Jane, the office manager back then, and she said they'd tried that concept once. It didn't work, and, in the end, it made the company look bad, and they lost a couple clients. I'll never share an idea again. They'd tried it way before I was hired," but I ended up looking bad, anyway."

After lunch, you reflect on the discussion, and the idea that once felt as if it would be helpful to clients now needs more consideration. "I'm the newest employee in the group," you mumble to yourself. "What makes me think I can come up with an idea that would be helpful or that others on the team haven't already thought of?"

You keep mulling over the idea during the drive home and as you cook dinner. This is silly, you think, who do I think I am? The company has been running just fine for the last seven years. As you slice carrots, the knife slips, and you cut your finger. Not deep enough to need stitches, but you grab a Band-Aid out of the drawer to hold it closed to stop the bleeding. Out loud you say, "I'm such a bumbler, I can't even slice a carrot without messing up, so what makes me think my ideas are worth a care."

You decide you'd best forget the idea and do the best you can with your current work tasks. Goodness knows, you are new, and others have been doing the same work for years. How ridiculous to think you could have a creative, new idea that would be helpful to the company. "Stay on task. Nose to the grindstone," you say. "Geez, I can't afford to get fired. I'm struggling to pay my bills as it is."

You create and get what you expect, believe, and concentrate on because you are directing God's Love energy through your thought-creativity as God, which is who you are.

Netflix has a category called Because You Watched This. It assumes that if you are into documentaries or horror stories or travel or cooking shows these shows are what you enjoy, so it lists more for you to watch and enjoy. Amazon does the same thing.

In a sense, this is what God's Love does. What you put out in your thoughts, actions, responses, and desires is what is created in your life. Then you get more of these creations, like Netflix assumes you want more of these movies or you'd change the channel. In a sense, it's taken as fact that this is the life you desire, the life you want to experience, just like giving you the Netflix shows it thinks you want to watch.

One of my favorite sayings is: "Expect the unexpected and expect it to be great!" This was from my stepdad, Abbott, who was an amazing teacher of positivity.

Since I've mentioned Abbot throughout, I'm inclined to tell this story. Way back when my brothers and I were teenagers, we came up with a nickname for Abbott—UBee — because we felt like he was a usurper as a dad. We would say: Ubee, would you like more potatoes? Or Ubee, do you want me to turn the lights off? I am chagrined to share that Ubee stood for, You Bastard (You B). At some point, he learned what it meant, but it didn't matter, because by then we learned he truly loved all of us (biological or not) and it had become an endearing name used for 40+ years.

Points to Ponder

- As you observe your thoughts, pay attention to thoughts about what you don't like and what you don't want, and then ask yourself if you see more of the "don'ts" than the "dos."
- How do you feel when the "don't wants" show up? If you "know" that life is hard, a hard life is what you'll see. Knowing is Seeing is a neutral force resulting in creating what you concentrate on and think about over and over.
- Use observation to flip on your happiness switch; gently let the thoughts of "I don't want" to focus on what you want to create through God's Love.
- Meditate on what gives you joy, give it your full attention, and welcome it into your life.

A Quick Reflection on Genetics

I often review my current life and decide what I love and what I'd like to change. Mostly I love it! This is funny and adds another odd tidbit of information. After a great deal of thought and self-analyzing, I've come to realize that the one thing I can't change about my life and myself is my height.

This may sound odd, but for the most part, you are in control of everything else. Your life circumstances are adjustable. You can educate yourself. You can change your mind and beliefs by knowing this is possible. And you can gain or lose weight, change your eye color with contact lenses, your hair with a cut or a bottle of dye, or have plastic surgery to get a new nose and chin or make wrinkles disappear. You can change your teeth with braces, like I did, or with dentures or implants. You can cut or grow your nails and make them a rainbow of colors. Yet, the one thing you have no control over is your height.

I have pondered this for years, assuming I would someday have a spiritual revelation about it. So far, anyway, that hasn't happened yet. But I know I'm a creator and in charge of the quality of my life. I will leave my height to God and to the genes of my parents.

Speaking of genes and DNA, when genetic testing became readily available, I learned Reyburn actually was my father. He was the father of all five of us with our mother Nancy. Surprisingly, he was also the father of two more kids, now adults, whose mother lived north of Duluth.

Another crazy coincidence. Yesterday, I typed about learning I had two brothers that I hadn't known about. One would have been conceived when I was two years old, and he passed away six years ago. The second brother would have been conceived when I was five years old and was given the same name, Jeff, as my second brother born about the same time. He passed away three days ago. In learning this and reading his obituary this morning, it stated he had a love of agates (just like me) and evidently spent a great deal of time looking for them at the water's edge and polishing them. I'm sorry I never got a chance to meet and get to know him and his brother.

QUESTIONS TO CONSIDER

1. What new perspectives are you discovering about yourself as you read this book?
2. How does changing your perspective impact your thoughts, moods, feelings, actions?
3. What is one outlook on life you would like to change to a new perspective?

Chapter 12

Creative Energy

Words give your thoughts energy. They create when you believe and repeat. Rather than flit from one thing to the next. Decide and stick to your desire. That is why it is so important to speak words that uplift, inspire, support, encourage, honor, respect, empower, energize, and celebrate.

At this point, I won't run through the concepts of being a creator again in some different form. It already makes me grin to think I've already explained the infinite concept of God in a few pages! That said, if any of this rings true, many other authors and teachers are in a much better position to add depth and greater understanding to this subject. That's why I listed a few of my favorite authors, speakers, and teachers at the end of the book.

Since you've come this far and are aware that you are God, it is up to you to turn inward and incorporate this awareness into your day-to-day life. You are a unique, individual expression of God, and you get to create what you want to experience in your life through your knowing. Or, you could say, since you create your life through thought, anyway, you might as well create what you want to experience.

Your mind is not a mere tool; it is a magnificent tool! Positive thoughts of what you want in your life can bring you joy and happiness and completely turn your life around. If you'd only think about what you want, and know it's already yours, your life would be amazing.

Your thoughts through the creative energy of God's Love bring about feelings, and those feelings bring about more thoughts. In a cycle, they go round and round, building on the original thought. When you become aware that you're not your body or thoughts, then you choose through knowing what you want in your life and focus only on that.

This is eye opening; the mind or its thoughts are limited. You think the mind is expansive, unlimited, and can be totally original. And, yet there are only three types of thoughts. All thoughts, everyone, fall into three categories: they all measure, compare, or describe. These three things are all the mind ever does. And these three types of thoughts are always in either the past or future. By the time you think or say something, it's in the past. To be in the present moment, you can only be aware and observe. Be present as God.

If you spent more time in the present moment, just being aware, your life would naturally become more joyous.

Your mind spin stories, and you believe them. Your life then begins to turn into that story, and you live it. Your mind creates the stories, you add the power of belief and then "knowing," and your mind is strengthened by your certainty, which then projects the details into the world or draws the elements into your world for you to experience. Your life today started with a story spun by your mind.

This cycles back to the biggest lie. Your mind has convinced you that you are only your body and mind. Because you have come to accept this as truth, it's then what you experience.

God, the real you, is the direct opposite of what the mind has been telling you and has convinced you is the truth. Yet, remember the facts mentioned earlier, thoughts can only be in the past or future. They reflect what has already happened or focus on what has yet to happen.

God can only be recognized and experienced in the present moment. It's what is right now. All that truly exists is the present moment and creation happens in the present. The past and future is the mind playing tricks as a form of mental self-importance or preservation, drawing you away from the present moment.

As I said earlier, there is no specific "when" in the future; it's fickle, and what changes it is "now."

Try as you might, you cannot find anything that didn't actually happen in the present moment. Or the present moment is where everything happens, and not in the past or future. Yet, there are no thoughts in the present moment. You are just aware. All thoughts are in the past or future and are limited to measuring, comparing, or describing.

It's mind boggling to realize that as much as 98% of your day is wrapped up in thoughts about what happened in the past or thoughts about what might happen in the future. Very little time is devoted to experiencing and focusing your attention on what is happening right now moment to moment.

This is the main reason you don't recognize God as who you truly are throughout your lifetime and back to the beginning of human life. God can only be recognized and experienced in the present moment; through your thoughts, the mind, which tries to govern you, is active only in the past and future.

You have allowed the mind to govern and control you

creating your life out of repeated thoughts based on the past or future, which are illusions.

There is only one moment—now—it is infinite God, who you are, and you can't be anywhere but in it. Yet, you are hiding in plain sight, covered over in the illusions of the past and future. You close your eyes to that fact and choose to hang out in the make-believe life of the past or future.

The past is memory, and the future is imagination. Neither type of thought has any existence outside of the realm of the mind and its thoughts. You make up mental stories based on your thoughts about the past and future, and, if you believe those thoughts and the stories they tell, they'll come true for you in present moment.

Positive Creation

God and Love's main goal is to please you, to give you what you want based on what you focus on. You control what manifests in your life by your thoughts and feelings, by what you know or believe to be true.

Here is the key. This is it! You are not thought that is aware of God. You are God that is aware of thought.

The whole purpose behind thought and the ability to think, and the reason it exists as a tool is to decide, order up, and create what you want. It isn't needed or useful for anything else because God has taken care of everything else. The sole purpose of thought is to give you what you want, what you think about, and emotionally dwell on. You are your personality, an individual, a unique creator, who has developed based on your personal experiences, and you choose and have created your life based on your thoughts.

Instead, "allow" miracles to happen rather than believe you need to "create" miracles. You're already miraculous. You are

God. You don't need to conger up anything. You must simply know it is real or already a reality and allow It to flow into your life. You often spend the majority of your time blocking the flow of this creativity by being hung up in the past or future, and you are blind to what has always been within you and who you truly are.

I explain a miracle as becoming aware and seeing more of your thought patterns come into reality than you usually see in your assumed, less significant, everyday consciousness. In other words, you become aware of something that was there all along, but you weren't aware of it, so you didn't experience it.

A good description of a miracle is "a recognized manifestation of God in your life." Yet, God's love is always active and flowing Its energy through Love's creativity. This said, sometimes it's blocked by the things you think, say, and do.

Being aware and miracle-minded, then, requires that you get out of the way. You block your awareness, so you don't see what is already there. Getting out of the way requires releasing old ideas and life-evolving habits that have not served who you really are, God as you. Getting out of the way takes recognizing the You who is powerful, whole, and ready to embrace this truth.

You are here on this planet, reading this at this time in order to open your heart to this understanding, and then to offer it to others. It's time to grasp that you are here in this body on purpose, and it's time for you to step forward and create the personal life and world you want.

Once you accept the truth of who you are, you'll create the life you desire and bring about profound changes. But your actions will add to the whole of life and help to heal the world through gratitude, joy, and positivity.

When you believe something, you are using the abilities of your mind. That is the action of thought, not to be confused with the knowing of God. When you know something to be true, you are expressing yourself as God. Guess which is more powerful? God is eternal and possesses all the spiritual knowledge available. There is nothing It doesn't know or hasn't experienced. It is all there is.

When you embrace the concept that your desires are already complete or answered and are a reality, you will no longer ask for something to appear or happen. Instead, you'll take on the "knowing" that the prayer, desire, or request has already happened or has been answered. By doing so, you attract the energy of completion rather than lack.

Points to Ponder

- Your mind is precious, but it's also a trickster that makes up stories you believe, because it has convinced you that you are your mind.
- Your mind likes to live in the past and the future, but if that's what you think about, what you had in the past is what you'll create in the future.
- God and God's Love want you to have your desires, based on what you concentrate on.
- God knows what you want based on where you put your attention and energy.
- What you call a miracle is a manifestation that you created, but now you recognize it and give it a name: miracle.
- We see profound changes when we focus on what we want and get out of our own way and pay attention to what appears.
- We don't have to pray for or ask for what we want, we only need to concentrate on it and know it already

exists and is on a path you recognize when it appears and follow as it unfolds.

Energy Flows Where Attention Goes

Starting at a young age, most of us were taught to pray for what we want, or for what we think we don't have. What we didn't know or learn is that God and God's Love work without needing our conscious understanding that or how they work. Plain and simple, it gives you what you focus on. So, if you work in unison with this creative power by thinking only about what you truly want, then God supports those desires rather than seeming to work against you. All along it has been giving you what you think about, so you need to refine your thoughts.

One of Love's laws is: "Energy flows where attention goes." This means this spiritual thought process doesn't necessarily understand the specifics of what you desire, dwell on, or pray for. It simply follows the path of energy you establish through your thoughts, and sometimes gives you what you don't want because for all the attention you gave to it, it thinks you've asked for it. Again, it doesn't understand words like "don't," but just follows your attention or energy.

Think of it this way, when you pray or desire something, or in order to receive something, let's say happiness. I want happiness. I need happiness. Bring me happiness. The underlying thought is that happiness does not already exist in your life. It is the "don't have" "not there" that the Love's creative thought hears, and then amplifies that desire or yearning.

God' goal is that you don't ask for what you want, but "feel" it's already there, and is the completion of the request or prayer. Or think of it like this: Rather than asking for happiness, become happiness. And, then everyday be grateful for the happiness in your life. To say, I am happy, thank you, is more powerful than saying "I want happiness." I need happiness isn't as powerful a statement as "I am truly grateful for my happiness!"

You will not enjoy lasting peace if you routinely switch and choose between happiness and disappointment. The only choice you really make is between truth and illusion. When you choose truth, you discover that happiness is always here in the present moment, whether you are aware of it or not. When you choose illusion and what you've created through past thoughts, you are in essence closing your eyes to what is right in front of you in the present moment. This is what it means to become aware of God and to wake up from the dream of separation. It's like opening your eyes and becoming aware of now.

God is never in danger by your dreams or mental closed-eye blindness. It remains whole and unchanged while you create your own world where lack, illness, pain, sadness, emotional suffering, hate, and fear appear to have the greatest meaning.

When you believe happiness, or any other desire, is already here, and you act as if it is true and present, even if you don't see it yet, then Love's creative power produces an energy field that literally pulls that desire into your life. It has to. Your feelings are the engine, but something else needs to steer the motor towards its destination. That driver is your mind. Creation doesn't come from your mind. It comes from the energy of your feelings, your attention, your focus, your love that is then directed by your mind. The mind focuses the energy, but the energy comes from your heart, from your sensed and spoken desires.

Your task in learning to create often begins with a belief that you are able to do so, and you already do it all the time. You may not recognize your creations as vividly obvious, but as mentioned before, the technology or process is exactly the same. You have had days or periods of time in your life when everything seems to flow perfectly, and little miracles occur all around you. This happens because you've connected with the God's Love process, though, perhaps, unconsciously, and you used it to attract what you "know" is already yours. You just didn't realize you were doing it. Now, all you need to do is intentionally focus that knowing and direct it toward what you want.

As you now know, for years I've focused on God's Love. It's what I call the process of acknowledging the awareness of God and the aspect of incorporating its creative energy within my life. Throughout the day, I mentally put heartfelt positive-energy bubbles around people and situations. I'm driven by this awareness and do my best every day to share this message in posting positive messages and uplifting thoughts in my option trading chatrooms and through kind words to everyone I meet. I have mentally incorporated the term God's Love within my writing about positive thinking and about trading options on the stock market (which I do to earn a living), so this brings me to the subject of Abundance. For some that concept is totally at odds with God. But not so…

Points to Ponder

When in doubt about your thought process and what you're manifesting, remind yourself: *Energy flows where attention goes.*

God's Love's produces your feelings that create an energy field that fuels the engine that the mind uses to bring what you desire into your life.

God remains whole and unchanged while you create, whether that's resentment and envy or love and generosity. God is All and Always.

QUESTIONS TO CONSIDER

1. Consider the saying, "Even no decision is a decision." What events are happening around you through indecision or no decisions?
2. What are three areas in your life that would benefit by applying energy and creativity?
3. What are three obstacles to finding and implementing creative energy and how can you overcome them?

Chapter 13

Abundance

Being thankful is one of the strongest and most transforming mindsets. It shifts your perspective from lack to abundance and allows you to focus on the good in your life, which in turn pulls more joy and goodness into your reality.

Let's jump in!

When it comes to listing personal concerns, most people say that financial abundance is at the top of the list. However, abundance comes in many forms and is not limited to the state of your finances, but whether you care to admit it or not, money and financial security relate to other areas of wellbeing. In other words, having your bills paid, while living in a comfortable home, without concern about food, transportation, or clothing, along with access to healthcare, all relate to financial abundance. In our society, employment and having retirement accounts or pensions, savings and investments is what is viewed as a secure, abundant life. And most likely you want to be sure you have cash in your wallet and money to donate to charities and causes or simply to help your family members.

Still, though you may want to enjoy greater abundance in

your life, negative thinking about money can repeatedly impact your financial situations. Changing your mindset is the most critical first step you can take for financial stability and a positive shift in your experience of abundance.

Your thoughts bring about feelings, and those feelings bring about more thoughts in a cycle that adds and builds on the original thought.

Consider this statement: "Okay, if I accept that I'm not truly only my body or mind, and I'm able to choose what I want my life to be by redirecting my thoughts, I'm going to tell you that it's hard to do when life is tough. I don't like my job. I struggle to pay my bills. I don't feel happy or appreciated most of the time. I feel like I am existing day-to-day, just doing the best I can."

It's easy to say that you ought to shift your mindset to be positive. On the other hand, when things are tough and you're robbing Peter to pay Paul, it's even easier to allow those negative events to overwhelm you and color your emotions and outlook, and to taint everything you think.

Not only that, but many of us start from having also been taught to think about money as sinister, even evil. You might think of people who have money (no particular definition of what amount or level constitutes "having money," by the way) as having negative traits of some kind, from despicable and manipulative to superior and holier-than-thou to selfish and self-serving.

Sure, it is acceptable to be paid a fair wage for work well done, but if you make money above the norm, then others might call you self-righteous and arrogant, "one of them," and likely, up to no good.

In many ways, to be poor and struggling to make ends meet might fit with an image of a down-to-earth, everyday person, who brings more respect and positive feelings than given a financially secure person. On the other hand, others blame the poor for their plight and seek to put them down even more. For the most part, these attitudes and perceptions (including the nuanced beliefs) could have been taught to you as a kid, and often modeled by the behavior and attitudes of adults around you. Misguided and even jealous family members might equate security with greed, or a wealthy person caught cheating is labeled "typical." Religious teachings can bias you for or against financial abundance, or good friends make a virtue of not having "too much," whatever that is. Negative ideas about money and the people who have it are liberally shared until the principles became so imbedded within you that you accept the beliefs as our own.

Abundance isn't a "woo-woo" term. True abundance pulls you into the present moment, so you recognize the true breadth of possibilities or the lack of them in your life. It's hard for most people to feel abundant when it comes to money because you're damn sure you'll never have enough of it. You may not be aware of your own financial hang-ups, negative beliefs and perhaps, neuroses. Without realizing that preconditioning and financial beliefs have caused you to expect to live a small financial life, you accept those circumstances as the way life is. At least the way your life is and the way it's likely to always be. You'd like to live a big life filled with mission and purpose, but your thoughts about money stay small. You get hung-up and stuck.

Abundance is the way out, the way to be unstuck. Abundance gives you the opportunity to break the habits mentally and emotionally that you've clung to out of fear and insecurity about your financial future. You stick to the knowledge, certain of lack. You're sure of it, and the way to break out of that certainty seems forbidden, or at least elusive.

But remember Knowing is Seeing. If you have imbedded a knowing of being poor and always having lack in your life, that's exactly what you'll see.

So, how do you change your thinking or prove to yourself

that you deserve to experience abundance? And what does this have to do with God?

Abundance is for every one of us. No exceptions. You may not know this until you've come to terms with your own financial story and discover you're getting in your own way. You are sabotaging yourself without realizing it. Your knowing that there is not enough, and your surety in a lack of abundance in all its forms, including financial abundance, draws the reality of lack to you.

So, the lack of abundance isn't a given or a forgone conclusion. Rather, it's your knowing, your belief in lack that manifests it. You are a creator. You always prove yourself to be right in your knowing. Whether you know or remember that you are God and God creates through thought, your personal firm "knowing" creates what plays out in your life. You don't realize that it is your concentrated thoughts and knowing that manifests your expectations. Then, as things play out as expected, it solidifies your sure "knowing" lack exists; it digs in and embeds itself even deeper. It becomes so fixed you will swear that it's true, the reality.

You tell yourself over and over that you knew you were right, that this is the way life is. And, sure enough, the situation plays out exactly as you expected. "What did I tell you?" you say to others and yourself. And, truly, you proved yourself exactly right. You got what you expected. You are the creator. You are God, creating life through your personal thoughts and knowing.

Albert Einstein said: No problem can be solved from the same consciousness that created it. We must learn to see the world anew."

When you think about this quote, you can see that you can't create abundance by staying in a consciousness of poverty, nor can you gain a sense of power in your life while identifying yourself as a victim who is down and out.

It's important to realize that God has given you control

through God's Love. You decide what you want to play out in your life through your thoughts and knowing, with or without understanding your own creative power. Until you accept that you have the ability to create and control what you bring into your life, you unknowingly create through your thoughts, beliefs and expectations, which have often been absorbed through other peoples' influences and your past experiences.

A simple practice to overcome this is to imagine that you have a box filled with everything you need or desire. In the box you see everything you want or think you need to make you happy or comfortable. You can take whatever you want out of the box, knowing that once you hold your desire in your hands, it is yours. You can also remind yourself that there is nothing that you currently lack or want that isn't at your fingertips. Holding it in your hands and knowing it is yours brings it into your life. Maintain that knowing until it happens.

To strengthen this concept is to understand that only you can satisfy yourself and knowing this gives you the power to fulfill your own needs and desires. When you search for gratification or fulfillment outside of yourself, it usually means that you are not giving yourself what you need to feel fulfilled. In that state, it's easier to follow a more negative or less satisfying path. Once you realize you hold the key to your own happiness, you will stop searching for things outside of yourself. You will reach into your box of plenty, draw out what you want, and know it will become a reality when the time is perfect.

So, now, ask yourself: What is abundance?

Abundance means needing less while having more.

You do the inner work of understanding and becoming aware of God and learning about all aspects of abundance, including your own behavior with money. In doing this work, you then free yourself from lack and what might be considered a haphazard or accidental financial life. You can become intentional with your creative desire for abundance in all its forms, including money.

Ask yourself what you truly desire in your life. Decide what is important to you. Give it some real thought. What really matters? And, if you had plenty of money and want for nothing, what would you choose to do with your life and your money? The answer will illuminate what you truly love and what is important to you. Your answer leads you to set priorities and goals and fill your life with joy and gratitude for the abundance surrounding you in all its forms, including financial abundance.

Abundance is a state of mind. It is a gift given by God. God is a part of everything, in everything, incorporates everything, flows through everything. It is you and me. It is in control of everything. This means you are in control of what is drawn to you because God is within you and has given you the ability to use the power of God's Love to create and draw in whatever you want. You are in control of what comes into your life because it comes through what you think, believe, desire, expect, and know.

Knowing is Seeing.

Points to Ponder

- God's Love created abundance in all things, including, but not limited to finances. Expand the meaning of abundance to include all you are and have and are surrounded with.
- To change your life, examine your beliefs about abundance, including money.
- If you believe lack is inevitable, then lack is what you'll see. To create abundance, change your beliefs.
- Choosing an abundant life is in your power—now. You as God create the abundance in all its forms.

- Lack is a limited state of mind. Unlimited abundance is all God, God's Love, and God's Spirit knows.

Abundance is a Natural Concept

Abundance means plenty, more than enough, or a very large quantity of something. The natural tendency of living things is to manifest, grow, and become more. Think about this for a moment. One single acorn holds within it the potential for an infinite number of oak trees and an even greater number of acorns. How about all the galaxies and trillions of stars? Cells infinitely reproduce and multiply. A pair of birds breed, creating thousands of birds. Love and kindness spread like a tidal wave. It is the tendency of nature to produce more and create more of everything. As mentioned, there are always new trees, new stars, and multiplying animals.

New things are constantly invented; new creations are produced, new things are built, new jobs are created, which grow businesses and expand cities. This happens because God is at the core of every person, and each person has a unique personality. One creation spurs new ideas. As it happens, you and I are God, so we have access to Its credit card with unlimited buying power. Decide what you want and know it is already yours. This is abundance!

Abundance is everywhere in the Universe, and it also appears in your personal life if you choose it or make a decision to be aware of it. In a sense, abundance is already in your life, but, perhaps, you aren't pleased with the form it's in. Maybe you see an abundance of negativity, fear, dislike, unkindness, drugs, alcohol, lack of respect, cruelty, illness, emotional distress, pain, disrespect, multiple failures, insecurity, a shortage of money, or an abundant lack of emotional support.

Again, I stress, through God's Love, you draw to you what you think about, say aloud, believe, expect, and know to be true.

Okay, let's get back to the positive concept of abundance.

The Universe continuously creates new things, and you are part of this abundance. If you feel lack of anything in your life, it is because of negative thoughts, expectations, and attitudes that block abundance. Instead, God's Love is drawing in plenty of what you believe and concentrate on. You are the creator. Thoughts and knowing create.

Think of realizing who and what you are as attitude. It is about knowing not doing. When you do something with a negative attitude, it then brings no light, not to you and not to the world.

Points to Ponder

- Abundance is God's natural state of being, creating, producing in cycles and without end.
- Know that you are a part of the never-ending creation of new things and renewal of all of life. Focus on what God's love brings to you without fail and see yourself as part of that flow.

What Do You Know to be True?

You are aware of the strong association between the term abundance and money. In the world today, wealth and lots of possessions are considered symbols of abundance. However, abundance can appear in many other ways.

Writer Remez Sasson has coined a phrase, "abundance consciousness." He defines this as "becoming aware of the existence of plenty of everything, of feeling it in our lives, and of connecting with it, even if it doesn't seem to be a part of our lives right at this moment."

Feeling and connecting is knowing that you are in control, and it is just a matter of knowing and drawing it to you through that thought, belief, and expectation. In other words, this God consciousness means feeling, believing, and knowing that you are a part of It, and It is already part of who you are and your life. It has given you the use of the Law of God's Love as a creative power.

Conscious abundance awareness opens your mind to see it around you and to recognize opportunities. Abundance consciousness breaks through the restrictive beliefs of your mind and opens your thoughts to a wider range of opportunities and an expanding point of view. It is a knowing without a shred of doubt that abundance is already a reality and, on its way, to manifesting in your life.

When you come to understand how you treat your money, you are reflecting how you measure your self-worth. You are choosing that which isn't changing in your life.

There are two main ways you might sabotage your finances on a regular basis. Let's use Avoidance and Addiction as our terms since I've been favoring "A" words—Awareness and Abundance.

The question is, do you practice either of these two?

When it comes to handling money, typical Avoidance behavior can look like this:

- You spend money as if there is no limit, and you do it to impress others. Gift buying is over the top in order to prove your wealth and generous nature to other people. Your spending is extravagant and can be on frivolous items.

- You pick up the check for every purchase or restaurant. You often brag about previous occasions of generosity, wanting it to be obvious that you are well-to-do and have a giving heart.
- Even if you can't afford it and don't need it, you buy nice things for yourself all the time. And, then sometimes, they remain in their box, unused and, eventually, get placed in a closet or given away. Yet, investing in yourself as a means to personal growth is a waste of money and effort.
- Credit card balances never get paid in full. The balances flow from month-to-month with minimum payments. You have a wallet full of cards. The credit card offers that come in the mail are routinely accepted as if the company is personally inviting you as a valued patron.

Generosity is intended to make you feel successful, rich and happy, but it seldom does. Money never stays in your wallet long enough to do anything productive with it. Although you're quick to spend, which brings you little enjoyment, you avoid giving this emotional need any thought.

Spending can be a way of making you feel special, buying love and needed attention. You underestimate your personal value with the hope that gifts will bring the love you need and desire. It's also a way to fool yourself into feeling you're generous and totally unselfish, and yet it's emotional need and insecurity that is the base of this behavior. Lots of people shop to celebrate.

For those who fail to understand their financial issues, abundance means spending money on non-essentials, which makes little sense. Abundance is about knowing you already have everything you need before it is ever needed.

It could be that by spending you are trying to fill a void

within yourself, yet if you take time to ask the question, you see deep within yourself that spending isn't the solution. You may notice how quickly the satisfaction and joy fade after your purchase, and how soon the urge to spend again appears. This is a symptom of disconnection from your true self as God, and that means the first step toward balance is a connection to your center and to who you truly are.

Digging deeper, if you feel down or perhaps think of yourself as insignificant when you're not spending money, you might have had a family member who believed abundance was equal to how much you could buy to show off to the world. Your family may have mishandled money, which helped to confirm the mistaken belief that you must spend your money while you have it in hand, or it will disappear tomorrow.

Perhaps, you have accepted this belief in your own way and have been busy sabotaging yourself.

On the other side of the equation, Addiction behavior can look like this:

- Quantity over quality. It is important to save for saving's sake. Being overly frugal or even, perhaps, stingy is a source of pride. Hoarding things can be a by-product of addiction. Surely, it will be needed one day. Waste not, want not. You can never have too much.
- Leisure or so-called me-time is a total waste. You refuse to go on vacations or a holiday, and spending money on things like restaurant meals is wasteful. Money spent on personal experiences, like an enriching seminar or class, exercise, meditation, relaxing me-time is useless and selfish. There is no greater value to a long, positive experience versus getting something done quickly and efficiently.

- Bargain hunting is a valuable endeavor and practice. To spend time at garage sales or searching for coupons has great personal value, certainly more so, than other financial activities, such as investing in education or personal growth to strengthen our earning potential.
- A job is a job. It is what people are being paid to do. You don't tip, period! No value is placed on people who have served you well, even when the service you received was above and beyond your expectations. After all, you know their employer pays them, so tipping is a wasteful expenditure.

If you express Addiction behavior, you are likely insecure about the value of your self-worth measured in any way other than its monetary value. You believe that the more money you have, the more important and valued you are, so you hang on to it like an addict.

Perhaps you were raised within a family who had to skimp and save to manage week-to-week. Or your family regularly put things and material goods ahead of you and other people.

I mentioned above that how you "treat your money" reflects how you measure your self-worth, not the amount of money itself. In other words, self-worth isn't—and can't be—measured in dollars and cents. It's an important distinction that addicted people have trouble understanding.

It's important to know and understand that your value is not based on the quantity of your money—it's not who you are.

Your personal story may be so embedded that you don't even know that you're playing your own movie over and over in your head. You are unaware that there are millions of other possibilities you could be living instead.

Mindset Makes the Difference

Abundance means knowing you have everything you need in this moment, no matter the challenges. It's a fair assessment and not based on your personal feelings or opinions. It means adopting a broad, generous mindset, not more stuff. It means sharing your wealth in such a way that creates more joy in the world for you and for others. It also means creating a balanced financial flow, in and out, that allows for a positive, secure, not uncertain, future.

Abundance doesn't mean that you should have it all. It means you already do.

The biggest danger with money, ironically, lies in its greatest value: It can be used for almost anything. You have so many choices.

Let's see if you can figure out how to avoid potential pitfalls.

Looking at a hypothetical example, let's say you feel stuck in the same routine, which makes it seem as if you are spinning your wheels and not making any sort of progress. It might be that because there are no obvious changes happening in your life, things always seem stuck, ordinary, and endless. But, if you take a moment to realize your life is constantly flowing and changing, you might discover there is a great deal of variety and change surrounding you. This could impart a new sense of excitement. Perhaps, today you decide to make a point to observe the things that seem ordinary—your home, work, neighborhood, nature, the view out your window—really examine these things and situations. Taking the time to look at the things that seem boring and unchanging could help you understand that nothing remains the same, and everything is always changing.

A simple way to get started is to pay attention to scenery through a nearby window. The color and movement of the bark and leaves on trees, or the birds, flowers, and people walking by with their dogs and their unconscious movements and expressions. Maybe you see the sky filled with clouds or just a scattering that change color second by second. It's truly surprising how repeating a ritual of observation can expand your awareness of change.

I intentionally pay attention to my mountain view and its variations every day. I never take it for granted. I have come to feel as if it's putting on a performance that changes every day as I take time to observe and appreciate the beauty.

Modern life compels you to be in a hurry. You feel pressured to make the most of every minute of the day. But this often means the activities that sustain you, uplift and refresh you, and help you expand your awareness are often the first to be sacrificed when you're rushed or face new chores or responsibilities that eat up our time.

This is why you need to remind yourself that there is more to life than achievements and making money. This is true even when you offer to care for others. On your list of priorities, your spiritual needs should occupy an important spot.

Each event and task you undertake and each relationship you manage draws from your energy pool. Taking the time to engage in personal nurturing and fulfilling activities refills that pool and restores you to thrive into another day. So, you not only make the time, but follow through and take that time for activities that add to your personal well-being. By the way, this has little to do with being selfish and everything to do with being aware of your needs. Routinely taking time to focus on what you really want confirms that you value yourself. Spending time with your thoughts, leads to tranquility and expands your understanding of what you truly desire.

It's easy to avoid using free time for personal pleasure or growth, because something always seems more important and pressing. You may feel guilty when you fill your free time pursuing personal desires and interests. Focusing on you can lead to the sense that you're neglecting your family, or chores, or perhaps your job. To carve out personal time, you may need to say no to other people's requests or refuse to take on extra responsibilities.

That said, scheduling 15 or 30 minutes a day for spiritually refreshing yourself can help you feel calm while it also gives you an energy boost. It most certainly allows you to be more in touch with God. Some people choose silent meditation or journaling; others prefer spending a few minutes outside, perhaps, intentionally doing walking. Reading, listening to an audiobook or music, drawing, or sketching, or engaging in any other practices that uplifts you makes good use of this time.

Taking time to nurture yourself may require sacrificing other less important chores or activities. The more time you commit to caring for yourself, the happier and more relaxed you become. The time you devote to yourself and nourish your spirit will revitalize you and help create a more balanced life. Overall, this helps you uplift others through just being who you are and living in your positive energy.

Giving yourself me-time helps you expand. In a way, this is how you become one with change, because change is the only constant in your life. You often want change because you're unhappy with the way things are in your life at the moment, and you then tend to focus on one thing that seems to be always present. You can change that, however. If you raise your awareness of the wide range of things you're exposed to daily, new stimulation will shake you out of your fixation on that one thing. You'll find joy in the ever-changing and unexpected happenings around you, which in turn energizes you and expands your awareness and acceptance of new opportunities—and simple pleasures.

It's important to take time for yourself, but to also pay attention to the breadth and depth of what surrounds you every day.

This is the way you come to a greater appreciation for the wide range of things present in your life.

Points to Ponder

- Expand your definition of abundance—life is about more than acquiring more material things.
- Make an expansive list of the different kinds of abundance in your life. Keep expanding that list—you will soon discover that you have no need to ask for abundance, you already have it and need only recognize it.

The Gift of Appreciation

Being acknowledged by others is a type of abundance you likely don't often think about. But when you allow others to appreciate you, you're receiving abundance. Gratitude, acceptance, acknowledgment, praise, appreciation, and compliments are all forms of abundance. You absorb honor when you recognize and let those expressions into your life. Pleasure comes from knowing you and your efforts make a difference in other peoples' lives. Savor these moments when those around you recognize and appreciate what you bring to the table. Their expressions of gratitude cycle back the good you have shared with them. Now they appreciate your expression. So, by accepting appreciation, your life grows even more abundant.

Maybe you don't believe you're an essential part of the abundance of God's vastness. Why is that? Likely it's because you don't let yourself think in unlimited ways. You limit your thoughts to the things that exist in your life right now. That means you aren't expanding your vision and outlook to, perhaps, the unexpected and greater opportunities that you may not be able to see yet. With limited vision, you may miss what you could draw into your life.

As I write this book and have mental conversations with you, I'm pouring as much positive energy and knowing into each word as I possibly can. I'm fixated on the certainty that it will help change and improve your life, as well as the lives of others. It hasn't yet happened as I write, but I am creating that reality, and I know it will. Knowing is seeing!

I've heard it said that every problem is mental, and every solution is spiritual. Based on God and God's Love this is true.

Vast abundance exists in God, and everyone is part of It, no matter where you live, and regardless of your situation and circumstances. We are God. God is you and me. To participate in this wealth and richness, you just need to open your mind to it, feel it, and expect it.

Remember: Expect the unexpected and expect it to be awesome!

Creative Visualization

You have no scarcity of techniques and tools to open your mind to prosperity, richness, and plenty and to attract those beliefs and eventual "knowing" into your life. Visualization is one of the best known and most useful tools—and it's free and doesn't require special training. It's a matter of cause and effect: What you repeatedly imagine in your mind and bring love to, you ultimately achieve.

Right now, you can come up with examples that prove this to yourself. Without doubt, you have experienced times in which you thought of something, played it over and over in your mind, and then, it happened. Then you say, "I knew that's what was going to happen!"

You'll notice that I didn't describe the thing you played over in your mind as good or bad. It doesn't matter. Whatever it was, you added thought energy or mental power to it, along with emotions, and you helped create it.

I have an exercise I do twice a day. I have a polished agate stone on my nightstand next to my bed. When I wake up in the morning, I sit on the side of the bed, rub the agate and run through all the things I'm thankful for. I often list family members, my home, health, and eventually, I come to the events that haven't yet happened. I express gratitude for events or fulfilled desires that may happen later in the day. I'm grateful for a successful meeting, for being able to express myself clearly, to be able to help option trading students learn what I have to share, to find everything I need at the grocery store. I'm grateful for my car that always runs well, for the rain to hold off until I arrive, and for the great parking spot, and so on. I'll often mentally create a pool of forgiveness in advance in case I need it, which it usually isn't. But if I get irritated at the person who carelessly pulls out in front of me without looking, I can draw from my forgiveness pool and avoid getting frazzled and bringing negativity to me. I start the day being thankful in advance because I expect perfect outcomes.

Then, in the evening, I again rub the smooth stone, concentrating my thoughts and intentions to thank God for all the people, events, and things I am grateful for that happened throughout the day. I fill my day with gratitude, forgiveness, positive expectations, and love.

Repeating affirmations is another way to help manifest abundance in your life. These positive statements can open the gate to prosperity, which is why I use this practice and share it with others. Weekly, I post a positive abundance thought in my option trading chatrooms and encourage traders to repeat the saying several times a day for a week. Then, the next week I move on to a new thought about abundance.

At the end of the book, I added a list of affirmations I've read and appreciated, and some of my own. You'll find them just before my list of other authors, teachers, and speakers I recommend.

Studying and repeating these sayings attracts new opportunities and brings the things you want into your life.

Points to Ponder

- Creative visualization is a tool that helps you focus on what you want, and only on what you want.
- You can practice visualization during the time you set aside for meditation and your spiritual practices, or you can do quick visualizations throughout your day.
- Affirmations also direction attention to what you want and allow energy will flow to what your thoughts create.

QUESTIONS TO CONSIDER

1. Define abundance.
2. What is lacking in your life that you would like more of?

3. How can you change your mindset to attract more abundance?

Chapter 14

Finding Time for Self-Care

When you start this positive dialogue and start taking care of yourself, you start feeling better. You start looking better. You start to draw better things to you. It all starts with you.

Ironically, when you get busy, likely the first thing that tends to get cut from your day is your personal spiritual practices, like meditation or journaling, or my morning and evening prayer rituals. Life feels complicated, so it seems to make sense to cut the "nonessentials" when you have less time and full plates. In the end, cutting self-care/spiritual corners doesn't help you or extend your day. Based on experience, you likely know that you function much better when you give yourself time each day to sit in silence to mediate, give thanks, or give yourself a little personal time. The busier you get, the more you need that quiet time for the day ahead. So, it may sound counterproductive at first, but during busy times you need to spend more time in meditation, not less. By being quiet and listening to God and being thankful, you'll be given what you need to get through your day, and it will play out the way you want or the way you have projected.

Just Ten Minutes Makes All the Difference

Adding just ten minutes to your morning routine for meditation can make a big difference, as can the addition of short meditative breaks in your daily schedule. The truth is, no matter how busy you are, unless you're in crisis, you always have five or ten minutes to spare. The key is to convince yourself that spending that time in meditation is the most rewarding choice. After all, you tell yourself you could be getting the dishes done or heading into work earlier instead. That is exactly why it's important that you learn to place high value on this personal time in the midst of all the other things competing for your attention. So, all you must do to discover that meditating more works to your advantage when you are busy is to try it.

You can start by creating more time in the morning. You could get up earlier, prepare breakfast the night before, take a few extra minutes before jumping into the shower or downing that first cup of coffee. You can also add short breaks into your schedule, from five minutes before or after lunch, to a meditation at night before you go to sleep. From a place of being centered and calm, you are more effective in handling busy schedules and keeping all the daily hustle-bustle in perspective. If more time in meditation means less time feeling anxious, panicky, stressed, and overwhelmed, then it's certainly worth changing your schedule a little.

Over the last twelve years, I have taught thousands of individuals to trade options, and I know some have not succeeded and have given up after they got started. Most didn't quit because of the outcome of their trades, but because of self-sabotaging beliefs and self-doubt. This is the reason I've dedicated so much time in explaining the importance of making a positive shift in our understanding about expectations and knowing. I want the same for all of us. "I" Am God. "You" and "I" are God, and we can create the lives we desire.

As I wrap this section up, know that I love you, just as I love myself, and I wish you the very best.

God is in you and Its creative ability through God's Love is available to you. You are a creator. The shape of God is the life you journey through as you structure who you are and who you decide to become.

Points to Ponder

- Make self-care a priority, no matter what. You will never regret it.
- Ten minutes of centering, visualization, and affirmation will pay off in your day many times over.
- Self-care increases your awareness of who you really are and allows you to avoid being caught up in the stresses of your day.

QUESTIONS TO CONSIDER

1. What are three areas in your life that would benefit from self-care?
2. What acts of self-care make you feel most nurtured and energized?

3. Sometimes, we need to let go of old practices to make way for new, healthier, more beneficial actions. What are three old practices you could release to make time for self-care?

Chapter 15

Generate Health

Good health is true wealth.

Before I delve deeply into this section, I want to open up and share something I don't often talk about. I don't like adding energy to it, but, in this case, I believe it's important. Earlier, I shared some of the challenging events of my early life. I also mentioned that I've been on a quest of learning what life is all about and ways we can control what happens within our lives and how it can play out. I've been asking these questions for more than 40 years. The answers have come slowly in bits and pieces.

The most recent and final layers of that search have been revealed to me and they relate to health. Over a period of five years, I was diagnosed with five different and rather unusual cancers, one not necessarily connected to another. These diagnoses resulted in major surgeries, plus months and months of chemotherapy and radiation over and over again.

I did what was necessary, and also tried to keep working. I maintained an attitude that I'm handling this, doing the best I can. I stressed that I'm strong enough to weather whatever comes my way. I was probably cocky. In a sense, I mentally said: Bring it on, I'm tough enough to handle anything tossed my way.

I see now as I mentally dwelled on the disease and my inner strength and ability to overcome, I was likely projecting a love of the victory. Likely, I was asking God's Love to give me more and more of what I was ready, willing, and able to conquer to prove myself to be a victorious fighter. In a sense, it was like a wrestler winning a match, and, once that victory happens, the wrestler doesn't quit wrestling, he looks for the next opponent.

Let's be clear. In no way am I suggesting God's Love was saying, "Okay, we will show this cocky girl. Let's give her another cancer to wear her down." I am saying I was concentrating on the battle and derived a sense of pleasure in the fight and ultimate victory.

Once again, I showed myself that the process of creation through God and God's Love is the same for all things, whether the ultimate goal is to bring something into our lives or to get rid of something negative.

If you have something you wish to get rid of, or anything negative you wish to remove from your life, you must focus on what you want instead. This means you should visualize and imagine yourself without that negative element right now. Instead, imagine yourself in as many scenes as you can mentally create where the unwanted negativity isn't there. It's absent. Imagine yourself free and happy. Eliminate any picture in your mind of the negative element or situation. Exclusively imagine yourself in the state you want to be in and feel that truth within you right now.

After meditating and lots of self-probing thought, I realized many of the experiences I mentioned earlier throughout my early life affected my personality development. Yes, I not only created a strong personality that defined me as a person not easily intimidated, but also, someone ready to tackle new ventures. With that came a tough inner bravado that led to the "bring it on" attitude, along with guiding self-talk like: I've got this…I like a good fight…I won't back down.

I don't often talk about my bout with cancer. Even many of my friends don't know because, at this point, I don't want to add energy to this area of my life. It's done and gone. Numerous times a day, I affirm how thankful I am for my perfect health.

I am sharing this information, so you can see I'm just like everyone else. I've created a life with challenges, sacrifices, hardships, hard work, as well as happiness and joy.

Over the last few years, I've been disease free. Physicians shake their heads in amazement. I concentrate my energy on what I want in my life, and at the top of my list is a strong body in perfect health.

One more note. I mentioned buying a second house in Asheville that was relatively close to the gift shop we owned at the time. This house was also within two miles or so of the cancer center where I went numerous times a week for treatment. The cabin on top of the mountain where I live and have lived most of the time is nearly an hour away. This is just one more example of how we create our lives, and then the puzzle pieces fit together.

Consider that both emotional and physical pain are signals, letting you know you need to stop and pay attention to what you are feeling. When you feel pain, often your first thought is to get rid of it by taking some medication. This is a logical response, but, sometimes, as you hurry to get rid of the pain, you forget that it's the body communicating with you and telling you it needs your attention. A headache can let you know the body is hungry and you need to eat in the same way that a sore muscle may be saying you need to exercise more often or back off to let the muscle recover from strain. If you ignore these messages instead of acknowledging the information, you risk having the condition worsen. At the same time, you create disconnection between your mind and your body.

Physical aches and pains are not the only aliments that let you know you should be paying attention to your body. Emotional pain also provides valuable information about your psyche, sharing that you have been affected by something and you'd benefit if you'd focus your awareness inward. In the same way you attend to a cut on your hand by cleaning and bandaging it, you need to treat emotional pain or a broken heart by being kind and surrounding yourself with love and support.

In situations like this, if you listen to your pain, you'll know what to do to heal yourself. It can be natural to resist pain whether it is physical or emotional, but once you understand it's providing valuable information, you can relax and take the needed time to listen before you reach for medicine. Sometimes, it's enough just to notice the pain. It will dissipate because its message was heard. Often, you reach for the medicine bottle because you're afraid that if you don't take it, the pain will never go away. Sometimes, healing comes with just listening and responding.

The next time you feel pain, emotional or physical, you might want to listen to your inner voice about how to relieve it. Maybe a few deep breaths will end a headache or sharing feelings with a friend or family member will ease heartache. Stretching and shaking the feeling off may help or a few minutes of meditation might be all that's needed. In the end, pain is sharing the message and drawing attention to it and its need to be healed.

Perhaps, you find it difficult to stay aware of health consciousness and being thankful for perfect health because you get snagged by the ups and downs of your daily personal experiences. Remember, though, it isn't just about you; it is also about the world. It, too, has ups and downs, ebbs and flows, expands and contracts, gives and takes, and these positive/negative swings affect you and can suggest your feelings aren't reliable.

If you only feel grateful when life gives you what you want, this is not true thankfulness. No one is totally safe from the twists and turns of everyday events, which can at any time take away your possessions, loved ones, and the situations you love. These twists and losses happen because you may have created some of these events in the past; or, because you are involved and connected to other people, you can be affected by their choices and beliefs. If you allow it, you can certainly be influenced by what other people create in their lives. Sometimes, it's these kinds of losses that not only severely shake you up, but also awakens a thankfulness that goes deeper than simply being grateful when things improve and go your way. Illness and avoided accidents can also serve as wake-up calls to the deeper realization that you are blessed to be alive and are truly becoming more aware of who you truly are.

You don't have to wait to be shaken up to become aware of the benefit of being truly thankful for all the experiences in your life, good or bad. Again, being fully present in the moment can do wonders in connecting you to unconditional gratitude for God and the life-creating force of God's Love that flows through you regardless of your current circumstances.

When you're ill, it's hard for the illness not to be all consuming. It's all you think about while you're mentally fatigued, weak, and in pain. It's so easy to give into it. It affects life on every level, and yet, you need to rise above it, understanding that it was created by events, thoughts, beliefs, circumstances, emotions, or feelings stemming from the past.

Beyond physically doing what you can, such as following doctors' recommendations, you need to switch your focus away from illness and concentrate on health. Be happy for perfect health even before it takes place. See yourself benefiting from perfect treatments that produce a healthy body that's easy to maintain. "Know" you are healthy. See it in your mind as being true. Believe it! Know it! Knowing is Seeing!

Eight Steps to Perfect Health

I am going to lay out what I call the Eight Steps to Perfect Health.

1. Destiny of Choice
2. Be Aware now! Welcome it! Let it go!
3. Imagine and Desire
4. Give and Share Compassion
5. Mind Over Matter
6. Gratitude
7. Joy-Fun-Play
8. You and God's Love

At about age three or four, you started storing memories and then God rose. This allowed your personality to develop, and you also begin to suppress and bury countless negative or bad feelings, which were then stored for your entire life in your subconscious mind. These feelings deplete energy, color your responses, and infect your life with their negativity and self-defeating bias.

Those feelings periodically rise and come to the surface, causing a commotion as they have an impact on new situations that then reinforce the belief that those feelings are real. Eventually, they become buried again, taking up even more space since they have multiplied and been validated.

It is this trapped energy that plays havoc on your health and the everyday circumstances of your life. It colors your thoughts and adds energy to what you draw into your life.

Negative emotions are the only feelings you hold inside. It's like a pool you have stocked with rare, prized fish you expect to view once in a while. The anger or hate or criticism you sense when you feel those negative emotions are the very same suppressed feelings that you have tucked deep inside of you.

Negative feelings create negative thoughts, and those thoughts become attached to earlier negative feelings. The pool gets deeper and deeper and filled with more and more fish. Those negative thoughts and feelings keep replenishing themselves, which, in a perpetuating fashion, keeps you from realizing who and what you truly are as a creator.

It takes a conscious effort to release the negative feelings from the pool. You can't ignore them and hope they will go away, or assume they're gone just because they're not present at the moment. They're suppressed in the mind, and, when something connected or similar happens or is said, the water will rise like a storm that dumps a surge of rain.

Many people believe that expressing these emotions is releasing them. The opposite is true. Releasing steam or venting is not the answer. That negative expression adds even more water to the growing pool, and as a result it deepens.

At other times, you think suppressing or hiding your bad feelings, tucking them away and trying to ignore them, will make them disappear. Not so. They're never really gone. You have stored them away, and that, too, adds to the deepening pool of negativity.

You're primed and ready to blame others or specific events for making you feel bad. It's their fault. Yet, if it weren't for your suppressed feelings, you wouldn't associate that event in that same way. Your triggers are set and ready to explode. It's because you are fearful that specific events bring up negative emotions. Said another way, it's because you have suppressed fear, shame, hurt, irritation, annoyance, impatience, hate, disappointment, self-consciousness, humiliation, sadness, blame, disillusionment, or any other negative feeling or state, that the current circumstance rekindles the past and brings up the connected emotions to be experienced again.

Suppressed emotional pain, hurt feelings, and negativity in its many forms can only be withheld for so long before it affects the body and brings on weakness, physical susceptibility, and disease.

You are often oblivious to your own creations and blame family, genetics /heredity, environments, nature, workplace contacts or conditions, rare mystery exposures, chemicals, weak organs or glands, and other causes for the diseases and illnesses that crop up. You never realize you are the creator or have brought on the physical weakness that made you vulnerable.

Don't dwell on the reasons behind the creation of the injury, illness, or disease. Focus instead on repair, returning to and maintaining perfect health. Again, knowing is seeing! Know you have perfect health!

Points to Ponder

- Internalize the eight steps to perfect health and absorb the reality that you are in charge of your health.
- Without judgment, gently note your negative emotions and thought/feeling patterns that take you away from knowing you as God's Love have perfect health.

Destiny of Choice

Whenever you next feel a negative emotion sweeping over you, no matter how it appears, you are experiencing this because it's already inside of you. It's not because an outside person or situation caused it. It's your reaction to the person or event that causes negative feelings.

Rather than declaring, "I am sad," or "I am really mad," you could take a healthier approach and say: "At this moment, a feeling of sadness or anger is flowing through me." If you just let the feeling flow, you're taking a stand of knowing you're creating through God's Love because you are God, and you are identifying with what is real and not the emotions flowing through you.

This response allows the feelings to pass and not be retained in your body. You are no longer adding fish to the pool.

Another way to handle a negative situation is to ask if you are the feeling of anger or sadness or are you the one who is aware of the anger or sadness?

"I am mad," or "I am sad," are more than simple phrases because you were here before the anger or sadness came. You will be here after the anger or sadness leaves. It is not who you are. "Am" means it is you, and you are not it. That is how you internalize those otherwise temporary, passing feelings. So, let anger or sadness pass through without adding energy or power to it.

Let's run through these statements quickly and note whether any apply. If anything resonates, you'll know where you need to redirect your thoughts.

1. The smallest things cause you to overthink. You get hung up on one thought for hours, mulling it over and over.
2. You have trouble falling asleep because of anxiety, even if you are tired.
3. You always imagine the worst in every situation.
4. You reject invitations even if you want to go out because you worry that you will screw up, letting yourself and others down.

5. You're scared about saying something wrong or dumb.
6. You dread and get nervous thinking about the future.
7. You always compare yourself to others.
8. You're always on guard because other peoples' opinions are very upsetting and set off your emotions.
9. You feel unwell physically and mentally most of the time.
10. You find it hard to forgive yourself for mistakes you make.

Examine anything that you connected with, and then make a different choice.

Remember, you are a creator. You are God, the creator of infinite miracles. Don't let the muck of feelings diminish the knowledge of who you are. Remind yourself, you are not your body or your feelings. Quit identifying yourself with your emotional responses. For every negative feeling that arises, question yourself and ask: "Am I that feeling or am I the one who is aware of that feeling?"

Observe or ignore negative feelings; it is your choice, just don't join in.

Soon, you will come to realize that it is God as you, who is aware of the feelings when they first appear; then they dissipate and are allowed to fade away. You are an observer. You can be aware and acknowledge the negative feelings, but you don't have to join in, and they will fade and float away like a morning mist.

In the twentieth century, you were taught mind over matter. In the twenty-first century, it should be God's Love over matter.

When asked what surprised him most about humanity, the Dalai Lama answered:

"Man sacrifices his health in order to make money. Then, he sacrifices money to recuperate his health. And then, he is so anxious about the future that he does not enjoy the present or the future; he lives as if he is never going to die and then, dies having never really lived."

Your objective ought to be to choose what you want to experience, and then, you will experience more of it.

Be Aware Right Now! Welcome It! Let Go of the Past and Future!

The idea that your life will be much better if someone else or a situation is different is an example of common, but misguided thinking. It can prevent you from creating happiness and satisfaction. You'll never be happy if you wait for the world to change based on your desires or expectations. It is you who must change how you feel by letting things pass and not internalizing negative feelings.

Feel it, even if it is sad or disturbing. Welcome the awareness, but don't internalize. Stand back, be aware, and then let it pass. Making the choice to let go of something is expressing power. Letting go is moving from feeling powerless to feeling powerful. This opens you to new possibilities.

Too often, you likely spend considerable time and energy trying to change the outside world and everything in it: spouses, friends, families, bosses, co-workers, and your so-called enemies. If only they'd change, you'd be so happy! It's a myth some live by.

The negative feelings are in you. No one has the power to make you unhappy. You allow them to come in, and you turn your power over to them. Negative feelings are self-inflicted. You allow other people in and absorb their thoughts and opinions like treasured items to preserve as if you're collecting precious gems to add to a cherished collection.

This is actually good news. The fact that you inflict negative emotions on yourself means that you can change it. You can stop doing it.

What you feel inside doesn't have to match your experiences in the outside world. Feelings are a magnet. They want recognition and to be expressed, which draws in more of the same type of feeling. Like attracts like. These feelings take energy to maintain. Happiness and joy are your natural God state, but negativity can cover it over.

If other people's opinions and feelings don't match yours, let them float on by. It's not your responsibility to change who others are and what they think and feel. Besides, trying to change another person doesn't work, anyway. As individuals, you must become aware and make your own changes. All you can do is be aware of others and the outside world and change yourself.

If, at any moment, you aren't happy, joyous, content, satisfied, or loving, then let the negative feelings dissolve and float on by. Then, you'll live the next moment, and if you keep up the process, all the moments that follow from your natural state of God are filled with contentment and joy.

Negativity offers safe shelter to even more negative feelings that settle in and nurture disease. That energy nestles into crevices of organs, muscle, tissue, veins, and vessels and weakens, contaminates, and causes deterioration and disease.

The key is to become aware when a negative emotion comes in. Then, don't suppress it, don't judge it, don't resist it, just recognize that it is a feeling. It is not your feeling; it isn't a part of you. It is only a temporary passerby. Don't try to change it or even to figure out where or what it comes from. If you don't resist it, it will just float on by. The energy will be released, and the feeling will disappear, causing no more damage.

You can do this every time you become aware of a negative feeling, and in that way, you don't add to it or strengthen it, because you've let it float on by. Occasions like this are opportunities to use your key phrase or (my "I Am") switch to snap yourself out of being negative and into a God mindset.

I know this is easy to say. I have a family member who, in my opinion, based on my assessment, isn't on a good path. But my opinion doesn't really count. If I worry, my concern doesn't help them; it doesn't change anything. I could fuss and point out what I see as their faults and bad decisions. I could do this until, as the saying goes, I'm blue in the face, and all it would do is add to my internal pool of negativity. The worry I feel, whether I express it or not, doesn't help them, and it poisons me. It settles in with other past concerns to further weaken areas that then develop into disease and poor health in me.

I've been there and done that, and I am not doing it again… if I can just let it pass.

In all likelihood, you have been mistakenly taught and have convinced yourself that if you resist expressing a negative feeling it will go away. It doesn't go away or disappear if you are still harboring it. It embeds itself in your body. It's in a closet, in storage, and starts to contaminate and bring about disease. It's guaranteed to reappear and to be experienced again and again. Eventually, its dwelling place will cause contamination and bring illness.

You have all heard the old saying, what you resist persists. Well, it's true.

If you concentrate on fear or the negative, placing your worry energy into the area of concern, you are in essence saying that this—worry—is what you want more of, and that's what you create.

Awareness is not the same as concentration. You can welcome the recognition of your emotions, positive and negative, and then let them float away and disappear. You can replace the emotions with gratitude for this process, your new understanding, and also for what you "know" you want in your life now.

As the feeling dissipates, it will also take some of the suppressed stored feelings with it to be released. Before long, all the closeted feelings will be gone and no longer drawing additional negative circumstances into your life to energize them.

By remaining present, being aware, and learning to disconnect from your emotions, you recover control of your energy supply and health. You no longer waste your energy by fueling the negative and infecting your body. Positive energy can now be used to enhance your life with health and the experiences you love and desire!

Be aware, welcome the realization of negativity, and then let it go.

Releasing negative feelings opens the opportunity to acknowledge and actively participate in being God, the Infinite Spirit you are and have always been, while experiencing life as healthy human being.

Points to Ponder

- No one has the power to make you experience negative emotions. You are in control of your moods and the flow of emotions that flow through you.
- You have the ability to observe the negative and positive emotions that come and go, and rather than resist them or put a fight to make them go away, ignore them, or negate them, you have the power to note them and direct attention to them or let them pass by.
- You are in charge of focusing on what you know you want in your life in this moment. You can choose where you direct your energy.

Imagine and Desire

Rather than just imagine, let's know you are not a drop within a whole, but a whole within a drop.

To solve any problem, take your energy away from it. Quit thinking about it, quit trying to fix it, quit giving it your attention, and quit trying to solve it. When you shift attention away from the problem, it will dissolve and fade away. It's like removing oxygen from a fire and watching it go out because without the oxygen it can no longer exist.

Instead, use your energy to replace the problem with what you want to happen or come into being as a replacement. Imagine and put your desire out there, knowing it will happen. Knowing is Seeing!

Abraham Hicks once said: "The Universe makes no distinction between the vibration you offer in response to what you are living and the vibration you offer in response to what you are imagining…"

Children play using their imagination. My two-year-old great-granddaughter excels at creating adventures in her sandbox. One episode after another plays out in which she's a mom, a doctor, a pet, a cook, a dancer, or another child. It may be hard to remember, but what did you dream of becoming when you grew up? I recall dreaming about and then building a treehouse that was my safe place. It led to wild pirate scenarios, cowgirl adventures, and other escapades. (I now have an adult treehouse.) What make-believe worlds did you create? What visions, spoken words, actions supported your desired reality?

As a kid you likely excelled at creating and exploring imagined realities, each rich in exotic images and sensory details. Immersing yourself in these realer-than-real adventures, you experienced different roles and life adventures, built social skills, solved emotional challenges, and enjoyed yourself.

Vivid imaginations are not just for children. Your imagination is powerful, multi-sensory creation tools you can use right now to intentionally create the life you desire. Through the creative energy of God's Love, whatever you give your attention to, dwell on or think about, whether it is something you desire to have in your life or not, is drawn to you.

The key is imagination powered by awareness, knowing you are God supercharges the creative process.

As Abraham Hicks stated, there is no difference between your offered vibrational response to what you are living and the vibrations you express in response to what you are imagining.

The key is to understand this and know you possess the power and ability to intentionally create the life you desire.

As an adult, I routinely watched the TV show Treehouse Master, with Pete Nelson, thinking it would be awesome to have a treehouse at the top of our mountain in North Carolina. This love of treehouses came from the childhood treehouse I built myself. One weekend, I took a leap and filled out a Treehouse Master online application to say I was interested in a treehouse. I promptly received a standard reply to say they had thousands of requests and had scheduled builds out five years or more.

I thought, oh, well, I'll hire a local builder. I wasn't discouraged or disappointed. The act of actually filling out and sending an application cemented my desire with commitment and a knowing that I would have a treehouse. A week and a half later a man from the Treehouse Master show called. It only took a minute for him to realize he had been given the wrong phone number to call about a treehouse that was already being built in Virginia. We talked for a few more minutes, laughed, and he asked about our property.

Three days later Pete Nelson called to say he had been told about our mountain and was going to be in Virginia in a week and would like to fly down and see our property. Pete Nelson came to design our treehouse about three weeks after I first reached out to them.

This is a perfect example about holding on to your desires, being positive about the outcome, and leaving the "how" up to God's Love.

As the power of thought, positivity, and believing has become a reality to me, I believe and am grateful for perfect health and knowing whatever I desire will become a reality.

If your life is not what you desire, then you have been creating by default, which is what you unknowingly do. You can easily begin through deliberate effort to create a new reality for yourself, including abundance and perfect health, starting where you are right now, even if that includes lack, loneliness, sickness, illness, or disease being experienced now.

Make these choices an important, meaningful routine in your daily life.

1. Begin to consciously recognize and acknowledge what you like and dislike and make a conscious effort to focus only on what you like and what you desire.
2. Devote a period of time every day to meditate on what you desire, lavishing attention in multi-sensory detail, and truly enjoy the imagining experience, the positive emotions of knowing you already have your desired experience. Imagine what it will feel like emotionally and physically. Will there be a scent? Wallow in the experience. Savor every minute. Feel it, cherish the joy. Know it is already a reality.
3. Cultivate joy, love, and thankfulness for every microscopic aspect of your life that you want to increase through offering your gratitude.
4. Dive in and focus on the "what" and "why" of your desires, and know God is orchestrating the how,

where, and when. Expect the unexpected and expect it to be great! Because Knowing is Seeing!

5. Develop an eager awareness of your emotions since they are an infallible indicator whether you are in line with what you truly desire or if you are fooling yourself by outside influences. If you feel good, you are on track with your desires.
6. Be grateful for the opportunity to exercise your free will as a God creator.
7. Play. Enjoy yourself! Have fun! Experience true joy!

Often, you find yourself caught up in your own rat race, trapped in the exhausting routine of your daily activities and the way you usually react, but with no known way to break free. Or perhaps life feels as if it's moving along smoothly, except for your relationships, financial situations, or physical health. And, then there are also your dreams, which are just out of reach.

Ask yourself what you are waiting for? You have the answer. Now empower yourself by understanding the key concepts of God and God's Love by learning the simple, yet powerful process of deliberately creating the life you desire through intentional expectation. You are supported by God. It is who you are. When you bring God's Love into the creative flow, well-being and abundance become the natural result. Life is easier, more satisfying, and joyful—and perfect health is the natural inevitable result.

Develop a "manifestation plan" by knowing what you want and knowing it is a reality as soon as you mentally commit to it.

Give and Share Compassion- With Yourself and Others

As you go through your days, you may be more conscious and accepting of the needs of others and are able to relate to them in an intimate and heartfelt way, more so than you can with your own needs. Sometimes it's easier to recognize the need to extend compassion to others, even strangers, more readily than you can give it to yourself. In other words, you are much harder on yourself than you are to other people, family members or strangers. The practice of compassion helps you evaluate your life. You can see there are times that you need compassion and recognize this tendency to be overly harsh with yourself. In those situations, apply kindness, understanding, acceptance, and forgiveness to yourself.

There may be people in your personal and professional communities who need assistance, friendship, or kindness, and they aren't able to receive it or feel it coming from their families or others. Perhaps, it is not being sent or they can't or don't experience it when it is expressed. If you can imagine what life is like in their shoes, you'll more easily be able to determine what they need and can give it to them. Even when your beliefs differ from those of other people, compassion leads you to appreciate and understand their logic or the source of their beliefs. Offering compassion, even when it's difficult, benefits both giver and receiver.

Empathy allows you to feel the pain of others, even when you do not share their hurt. This applies to conditions as well. You experience empathy when you see others in distress. In some situations, you can brush off rudeness or lashing out because empathy allows you to not take behavior personally. You can come to understand yourself better if you see the qualities in yourself that you see in the people that you are relating to with compassion. Empathy helps you to become closer to others and perhaps, to humanity at large, while also being gentler on yourself.

Recognizing what you need to change about you is an important practice. That quest can be done with compassion, though.

You can understand and alter behaviors, thoughts, and reactions without harsh judgment. In fact, being overly critical and hard on yourself contributes to overall negativity, which only means you've added layers to areas you want to change.

Collected negativity brings dis-ease and, eventually, disease.

Share and show compassion to everyone, including yourself.

Points to Ponder

- You as Infinite Spirit of God are empathy, compassion, forgiveness, and love. You need only reveal what is within you.
- Harshness and judgment toward yourself and others dissipate when we reveal compassion, empathy, and forgiveness along with an open heart that shares God's Spirit that is you, as you.

Mind Over Matter

The power of the mind is a wondrous thing because it is so strong, but it is also difficult to control. You can find yourself thinking one way, knowing this thought may be creating trouble for you, yet you find it impossible to stop and redirect your mind.

Perhaps, you judge your shortcomings harshly, especially if you're critically trying to achieve perfection. You think that criticizing yourself will somehow make you change, so next time you encounter X or Y you'll react differently. However, in the process of self-criticism, you beat yourself up over faults and failings and overlook your good qualities.

Fortunately, change doesn't have to come so hard if you accept that everyone makes mistakes. You also usually find that unsuccessful efforts can be steps in a learning process. Appreciate yourself for who you are, rather than for what you do or don't accomplish.

Do you realize that today you may or perhaps, not receive a phone call making you a great offer, compliments from strangers or friends, numerous emails, unexpected surprises, letters, visitors, or gifts? Also, today, you may or may not receive good or bad news. Do you realize today you may or may not encounter disputes or acceptance or agreement?

And you are the one who decides them all.

Once you recognize that successes and failures have little to do with your self-worth, you can be gentler in your self-appraisal. As for physical wellbeing, you can first start to notice your thoughts and your reaction to them. For example, many adults—and kids—get sick at the same time of year. You might be convinced you'll "catch" the flu or a sinus infection every October when the leaves start to fall. You may always get dizzy or feel faint when you get a shot or injection. Or you get a queasy stomach every time you fly in a plane. You may even be aware that your thinking has an impact on your experiences, yet you continue to think you'll get sick, and then you do. Now you've strengthened your knowing in this single area.

There are times that you develop symptoms to draw your awareness to something that needs your attention in order to process it or to move it through your body. However, when you're sick or exhausted because you don't exercise the creative healing power of your mind to aid your physical health, one of the mind's most important functions, you're misusing your creative abilities. You can use your mind to communicate with your body, yet you often think of the two as separate, which is the mind-body split. Despite many kinds of evidence to the contrary, you may believe one has little to do with the other.

If you try to get rid of illness by holding it in your mind, you are actually sustaining it with your energy. The only way to solve or correct a problem or condition is to let go of it and focus on what you want as a replacement. Be grateful for perfect health. Know you have it now, even if you don't yet experience it.

Ironically, you give your attention to what you don't want, expecting that your attention will change it. Go to the audiologist or optometrist if hearing or vision is giving you trouble. Do what needs to be done and then stop your concerned, negative attention and the problem will improve or dissolve. Routinely reaffirm what you do want. I am healthy. My hearing is excellent. I have perfect sight. My weight is just right for my height. I am loved. I am accepted for who I am. I am God, living life as me.

A negative thought is harmless until you believe it. Once believed, it resurfaces repeatedly, adding strength to your knowing until it becomes a reality. By letting go of negative thoughts as they surface, they will fade away and will be replaced by new positive thoughts about what you do want in your life. Focus on awareness, happiness, love, and what you desire.

It is as simple as this: Your thoughts and your knowing come back to you as your experiences, like expected friends who visit regularly.

You experience what you know because Knowing is Seeing!

It is knowing that has the power. Thoughts can come and go routinely. It is your knowing as you absorb them and take them in that creates their reality and power in your life.

You hold on to the things you know like precious treasures. They occupy your time, fill your days, disturb your sleep, and taint positive occasions. Those known beliefs make you sick, keep you poor, fill you with fear, cause anger to rise to the surface, make you tired, cause loneliness, destroy relationships, make you feel inferior, so much so you feel lousy, and then you feel like there is time for nothing else.

It is easier to release known beliefs when you come to understand that your "knowing(s)," all of them, have come from others. Since infancy, your parents, siblings, friends, TV, church, ministers, bosses, co-workers, teachers, society, government officials, and radio and TV dialogues have instilled their beliefs until they have become your own. The moment you believe what you've heard, it instantly is internalized into the subconscious mind to become active in your life and it will play out every chance it gets. This repetition solidifies your belief. Soon, you believe you know, and that's what you experience over and over again.

Become aware! Your subconscious mind runs your life if you let it. Pull yourself out of the tainted life your subconscious mind is creating and become aware of God, which is who you really are.

We've discussed releasing negative feelings by letting them dissolve and float away like a mist. Do the same with subconscious beliefs. You can release them, too, and they vanish from your life as you let them dissolve as you remain, strengthened to live your life as God.

Limitations of any type are negative beliefs. Release them. Who and what you are is unlimited. Lasting happiness, complete freedom, and perfect health will be revealed and experienced because it is no longer limited by false beliefs. You come to know you are God, and God is not limited in any way.

A knowing held for years, decades, or the better part of a lifetime with thousands of thoughts attached and supporting it, buried in the subconscious mind, can feel emotionally heavy and depressing. It can make you feel older, bring illness, or hold you back from living as you desire.

The effects of your past are ever-present in your now, so as they rise, forgive them by releasing. Let them float away without giving energy to them. Imagine a fog that floats by and leaves the surrounding landscape only lovingly touched by its presence.

Releasing these thoughts that are not needed and are detrimental would be like being an oak tree that lets the fog, and its breeze remove dead leaves.

A way to become aware of your known beliefs is to become aware of your reactions. When you react to something, anything, it's because you have a "knowing" buried within you that brings up that reaction. To notice or note a reaction is to become aware of it. Don't judge or respond to the reaction. Noting it is enough. Recognize that a reaction is what it is, and then let it fade away.

Beating yourself up about your reactions adds to them, which tends to lead you to hold on. Analyzing, judging, or condemning creates energy that clings to it, burying and shoving it down deeper. Or, put another way, participating in a reaction causes it to grow. Instead, awareness tends to lead you to say: I'm feeling angry. That's not me, not God. I'm grateful to be aware of this emotion. Let it fade away.

Replace the reaction with a positive one. I am happy. I am grateful.

Remember, the mind reacts to situations, not the real us, not God. Once an emotion or reaction is exposed, it loses its power and will disappear.

God dissolves everything that is not true, and what will be left is pure joy and gratitude for physical health, mental fitness, happiness, love, fulfillment, and ease. Whatever you want will find its way into your life, bringing more appreciation and joy.

As I said earlier, the goal of Knowing is Seeing is to point you into the direction of health and wholeness, but we can't do it for each other. No one can do it for another person. It's up to each of us to discover the path and follow it ourselves. There is nothing that someone else can make you believe. Consciously or unconsciously, before you accept that something is real, you must experience it. You then choose, false beliefs vanish and what you desire and "know" manifests, and God can be experienced in the present.

Becoming aware of your own creative abilities, you then have the power to create physical and mental health simply by paying attention to what your mind is repeating over and over. Once you hear and become aware of yourself and the performances you continually repeat, you have the option to let the recordings keep running or to make new CDs. Perhaps you'll create one in which you recite over and over that you have perfect health and abundance in all its aspects.

It can be said that you're like a tree and your growth depends upon your ability to soften, loosen your hold, allowing you to shed beliefs or habits you no longer need or that no longer serve you. This could sound odd if you think of a tree as rigidly structured.

Trees grow through their roots, trunk, and branches. They also grow wider with each passing year of age, creating the rings you see when a tree is cut down. As they continue to grow, they shed the bark that once served to protect them, but now it's no longer needed to help or contain them. This applies to you as well. You create boundaries, beliefs, and develop defenses to protect yourself, and then you outgrow them. This protection no longer serves you. Within a tree, this outer bark is composed of dead cells that protect inner tissues from disease, infection, and drying until they are no longer needed. If you don't allow yourself to shed those defensive "bark" layers, you can't expand to the full potential of who you really are.

Trees require their protective bark to expand and to allow the process of growth, which then permits renewal to take place. Cambium is an expandable single layer of cells that protects the new wood and inner bark. Likewise, you need your personal boundaries and choices to expand so that your more vulnerable areas can heal and unfold. But, overall, your growth depends on your ability to choose and accept who you really are, so that the more exposed parts of yourself can heal and then strengthen toward emotional and mental stability and perfect health. Your growth also depends on your ability to recognize, accept, and shed protective self-imposed limitations that are no longer needed like the outer layer of tree bark. Often, these layers of protection you've put into place to serve you, eventually become constricting.

So, you unconsciously set limits for yourself in the past, but now you can consciously cast off these limitations as if they are no longer needed layers of bark. This is how life will become an expanse of infinite opportunities. When you have allowed your mind to explore all the possibilities that exist through Infinite God, you never need to ask if your desires and dreams are possible. You need only ask yourself how you ought to go about realizing your dreams and ambitions. Decide what you want. Know that anything is possible and know it is a reality before it materializes. You are God and through the creativeness of God's Love everything desired is possible.

When you have emptied yourself of the previously believed doubts, fears, and restrictions that once held you back, insecurity and doubt can find no room in your mind. Your confidence becomes unlimited when encouraged by the knowing and creativity that lay deep within your true self, God, and you express your desires through God's Love. Its only function is to create.

Different from a tree, you must consciously decide when it's time to peel away the bark and expand yourself, so you can move into positive, more conscious personal growth. You set the boundaries of your personal desires and expansion. You grow and expand spiritually each time you shed a layer of self-consciousness or erase a limitation that restricts you and no longer serves. Symbolically, you become a bigger person by consciously choosing to be positive in your choices. In doing so, you create space for your next level of growth.

Speaking of trees, I mentioned my love of the mountains and the way in which a treehouse was built on the top of my property. So many people expressed the desire to spend a night in the treehouse that the vision expanded. I soon put the knowing out that I would find the right property, architect, and contractor to build a series of treehouses along with an event center. Step by step, even during the time of the Covid pandemic, the pieces slipped into place. I found a 95-acre piece of property. It was as if it had been set aside and held for me for five years. It had been attended to, but sat vacant, ready and waiting. It was beyond perfect. House renovations, gardens, a labyrinth, and treehouse construction have all taken place or are underway. Stony Woods Estate is a reality.

This project stands as a great example. Harness the power of the creative mind (God's Love) and choose supportive, knowing words and positive efforts that create what you desire, such as good health and joyful spirits. You remember to fertilize the field of your mind with attentive, loving, and nourishing elements, as if you're a tree growing larger and stronger. Or perhaps you're a master gardener, culling the weeds so the blossoms of abundance and perfect health will bloom.

Points to Ponder

- Examine beliefs about health other parts of your life you hold, perhaps in a knee-jerk kind of way: Flu season means…what? What is flu season anyway? I always get sick when…really? Why?
- If you focus on illness, illness is what you'll likely get. Passing negative thoughts have little power but observe where you put your attention.

- As you go through your day, note negative thoughts and old beliefs that come to you and know they aren't you. With compassion toward yourself, affirm who you are.
- Affirming health is not the same as ignoring symptoms that something is amiss. Take care of what you experience while you direct your focus to health.
- Focus on the fullness of what you want, rather than making mental lists of what your mind tells you is lacking. Be the fuel energizing peace, health, creativity, abundance, love, and more.

Gratitude

Being grateful is the equivalent of feeling the presence of God in your life. It's the same as being in a state of bliss.

To practice gratitude, you develop an optimistic attitude toward life. You don't ponder things you don't have; rather, you focus on being happy with the smallest things in your life, whether you possess them or not.

At times, you feel grateful without conscious effort. At other times, you need to intentionally increase the number of times you deliberately express gratitude. Practicing gratitude on a regular basis helps it to become a mental habit.

Routinely expressing gratitude helps with the following:

1. Thankfulness helps you to easily move through tough times.
2. When you appreciate, you become awestruck by all the goodness life has provided you.
3. Practicing gratitude improves mood and emotional well-being.

4. Routinely expressing gratitude helps you reflect and zero in on the things and happy situations you want to increase.
5. Gratitude builds positive emotions and personal interactions in nature, with people and while taking part in social occasions.
6. Appreciation or gratitude helps you to reflect, enjoy, and relive moments of happiness.
7. Gratitude helps you be present in the moment and not waste energy on the past and what you don't have.
8. Gratitude is a display of your positive feelings toward a person or thing. It is a loving emotional touch.
9. Gratitude can be expressed and described in many ways, including thankfulness, kindness, and unconditional appreciation and love.
10. Gratitude creates selflessness within you. You create your best self by expressing thankfulness.
11. Being grateful is an awesome, uplifting experience. It positively changes the way you perceive other people and situations touching your life.
12. Incorporating gratitude boosts optimism. By celebrating life, you sharpen your attention toward areas deserving thankfulness and gratitude and that you want to increase and nurture.
13. Gratitude develops boundaries and acceptance for healthy personal interactions.
14. Practicing gratitude for things you desire, brings them into reality.

Thank you! I appreciate you. I am grateful for perfect health. I am truly grateful for having money and the ability to obtain all the things I need and desire. I appreciate my wonderful, emotionally healthy relationships with family and friends. I enjoy work and appreciate my productive work environment…

Many people enjoy keeping a gratitude journal. Every day, perhaps routinely before going to bed, they write down ten, fifteen or twenty things they are grateful for that day.

I mentioned the small rock on my nightstand that I rub before sleep as I review the things I am grateful for. The next morning, I stroke the same stone expressing thankfulness for a great night sleep and for the perfect evolution of upcoming daily events, being grateful in advance for the positive outcome.

Points to Ponder

- Read and reread this discussion of gratitude.
- Notice the sensations in your body when you're filled with unlimited gratitude.
- Several times a day, stop to remind yourself to think or speak words of appreciation for your life.
- If you need more reminders and want to develop a gratitude practice, start with by keeping a gratitude journal—every day add to your list.

Fun-Play-Joy

The most basic point of life and living day-to-day is to feel and express joy. It's a two-sided coin. The objective is to experience joy for who you are and to have fun, play, and share joy with others.

Your worthiness to experience and share joy is not based on physical or emotional qualities or how much you have accomplished.

A great deal of who and what you are or feel evolves as your journey through life; however, your true worth is perpetual. The term "self-worth" is often used in the same way as "self-esteem," but these concepts are different. Self-esteem reflects how you feel about yourself in any given moment. Your worth is not a result of your intelligence, talent, looks, good deeds, or accomplishments. Worth is immeasurable and an unchanging creation of your eternal and infinite connection of your personal Spirit of God to God. It represents pillars of optimism and self-knowing. Your self-worth can't be taken from you or damaged in anyway, but it can be unfulfilled, overlooked, and disregarded.

By routinely recognizing your self-worth, however, you can ensure that you never forget what an important, cherished, and special embodiment of God you are.

You are born worthy of joy. Your worth is essential to your very being and who you really are. Your concept of your self-worth is supported by your thoughts and actions. Each time you strive to appreciate yourself, treat yourself kindly, establish your personal likes and dislikes, set boundaries, positively express your desires, and broaden your outlook, you express your true value.

During periods when you have lost sight of your self-worth, you often feel despondent, vulnerable, or lack confidence. You place energy in false areas of importance rather than directing it to the beauty and strength that resides within you. This misplaced energy compromises you mentally and physically, which then weakens you, so you draw in negativity, which opens the door to disease.

When you feel worthy, you immediately accept yourself. Self-worth as an individual, connected with all life and people on our planet, who are also God, allows you to be joyful and assured, determined to play, have fun, and express joy. This understanding brings you to know that self-worth is not based on just accomplishing your goals, but also allows you to view errors and shortcomings as just another part of your life's journey. These aren't a part of self-worth, and truly, mistakes and shortcomings need not be a part of self-esteem either.

Remember the earlier example of humans as drops of water in an infinite ocean. Your self-worth comes from being a separate individual or drop, along with being an integral part of something larger than yourself like the ocean. Building awareness of this concept can help you to express the tremendous worth within you through the expression of fun, play, and joy that promotes self-satisfaction, happiness, and perfect health.

God is happiness. Any time you experience happiness in your life, it's a glimpse of God, a peek, a quick view of the magnificence that you are. You are this happiness, not an object that brings happiness. The object is unimportant, irrelevant. It's part of what you called your physical life, but happiness and joy are real, and the essence aspect of what you are as God.

When you are happy, problems and difficulties tend to solve themselves. Health improves. It's as if the universe is conspiring on your behalf. This is laughable, because that's exactly what's happening as God and God's Love create as you and me and everyone else.

The happier you are, the more carefree and effortless your life become, which adds to your happiness, which then creates more and more ease and peace.

Points to Ponder

- Self-esteem is a mental evaluation unrelated to your worth. Self-esteem and self-worth aren't interchangeable concepts.
- You have inherent worth: You are a Drop of the Ocean we call God.

- God's worth is unchanging; likewise, your worth is unchanging. Nothing you say, do, think, or believe changes your inherent worth as God.

Us, You and Me, and God's Love

God's Love is the creative, unfailing process of thought and knowing.

When you feel lonely or isolated, you have lost the idea that we are all one and that none of us are separate from God, the Whole.

I'm sure you have had days when you feel lonely, but the concept of loneliness comes from the false belief that you are separate and isolated parts in a universe filled with other separate, solitary parts. In truth, you can be no more separate in your world than a bird can be separate from the air in which it flies or a fish from the water in which it swims. When you zero in on the boundaries you see as solid, they prove to be quite translucent. When examining how your skin is affected by changes in the quality of the air, scientists tell us it's not clear where your skin ends, and air begins. When air is dry, your skin becomes dry, and when it is humid and moist, your skin becomes damp and pliable.

In the same way, it's difficult to determine boundaries between one person and another, especially when our actions and reactions tie us together. Every move you make has an effect that touches all the people around you. The air moves through your movements. On an even subtler level, when you share space with another person, you pick up on their energy. You sense how they are feeling, and you often become aware of their emotional energy, whether you mean to or not.

This is what is meant when you say a mood or feeling is contagious. You can't help but be a part of other people's energy because you draw from the same energy field. This force unifies all life. In the broadest sense, this energy force is the spiritual force mystics and gurus encourage you to move toward. It's the source you will become a part of when your Spirit moves into it at the end of this physical life.

The bottom line is we are all one. We are all God, creating through God's Love.

There is no happiness out in the world because it's not outside of you in the first place but is in you. Happiness is often covered over by thoughts and beliefs that you have fooled yourself into believing. Happiness from material things and experiences come and go. The feeling is fleeting, which nudges you to move on to search for the next happy experience.

The lasting happiness you have convinced yourself is out in the world simply isn't there. Happiness is within you, where it has always been. It's within the Spirit of God at your core, who you truly are. This is the truth, despite false thoughts, mistaken beliefs, and misinterpretations.

Every person who has ever lived has been driven by the same goal and purpose—to be happy and to feel joy.

Everything you do, think, want, pray for, dream, strive for, work toward or against, or wish for comes from thinking it will make you happier for either not having it or having it. The desire for happiness is the single strongest motivating element behind every single thought and decision you make. That said, all these decisions bring you no closer to your happiness goal. Seemingly hidden at times by false beliefs, the happiness you seek has been present within you the whole time.

When happiness is believed to be on the outside, you fall prey to the habit of putting happiness on hold.

I'll be happy when my health improves. I'll be happy when I get a new job…or find the right partner. I'll be happy when I lose weight…or have a child or when the kids grow up.

I'll be happy when I earn more money. I'll be happy when I

have more strength... balance...stability...when I feel better... when I move.

You tell yourself you'll be happy with a new boss or when a co-worker quits. Or, maybe when the seasons change, or you own a house...or when you sell your house...

I'll be happy when I fall in love, or marry, or for sure, when I get divorced.

I'll be happy when I can travel or when I can stay in one place. I'll be happy when I make friends, have a new car, start a business or sell it.

I'll be happy when my house is renovated and when I'm healthy. Or I'll be happy when I earn forgiveness.

You can't attach happiness to an action, change, object, or distant time. You put your happiness on hold if you believe that happiness comes from things on the outside. You put happiness on hold as you wait for someone or something to come along to make you happy. Those things may come along for a moment and then quickly disperse like a morning fog. Lasting happiness cannot be found in external things. It is and has always been on the inside of you.

Think about something you have dreamed about and longed for, something that after a great deal of effort and drive finally happened. Did the happiness you expected linger and fill your life with everlasting joy?

A year or so after my husband Jack passed away, I decided I needed something to fill the empty, quiet hours in the evening when I wasn't working. I taught myself needle felting, where I take raw wool and use a long, barbed needle to push it into a piece of wool backing, so that the raw wool becomes like paint, and I create pictures of animals against a natural background. I look forward to and enjoy every minute I spend felting. This creative expression fills my evenings with joy.

Hours pass quickly while I'm immersed in thinking through

designs and creating. I needle felted several pieces and stored them in the closet when they were done. Before long I started to become practical, thinking it was foolish to spend so much time creating art pieces, only to tuck them away where they weren't seen and enjoyed. I started to hold back and spent less time felting until I figured out what to do with the created pieces, other than filling a closet shelf. I knew the answer would come.

My daughter mentioned my felting to a friend, who owns an arts and crafts shop. The owner called me out of the blue and asked if I was interested in participating in a month-long craft show they were having in one area of the shop, where she wanted to introduce new artists. God's Love created a way to share my work based on my thought energy. Within a week, every piece sold, and I also had a commission request.

This was amazing. The owner asked me to become a contributing artist at the shop, and I accepted. I hadn't completed too many new pieces before I felt the pressure to produce pieces quickly to fill my allotted space within the shop. What was once a relaxing, looked-forward-to pastime became work, where self-imposed pressure to produce took away the joy. Each evening, I pushed myself late into the night to complete a piece I could bring to the shop the next weekend. I felt an obligation to produce, and I began to dread the time I spent creating a few new pieces a week on top of working in my full-time business.

I have since returned to felting as a joy-filled hobby, only working when I feel inspired. After I complete a few pieces, I bring them to the shop, and they decide if they want to buy them. They don't sell for as high a price as I received earlier as a contributing artist, so in a sense, I am selling for wholesale prices. Still, I earn an amount above the cost of materials, which allows me to experiment with new techniques and to replace the wool.

Others enjoy my felted wool pieces, and I recaptured the joy spent in creative expression.

As I describe this life experience, it's easy to see the pattern that God's Love created through my thoughts. It brought forth a welcomed hobby, it then brought about a way to sell my work. When I accepted full-on production, it brought a level of distress and a shift in priorities that diminished my joy. Pressure turned my hobby into a second evening job. However, being grateful for the joy felting brought, plus being open to the right solution, allowed me to find a modified way to share my talent and express myself at my own pace. As a result, I once again have creative satisfaction and joy.

Throughout this process, I remained open and knew the right answer would come. I remained positive, and, though I didn't personally know the answer, I knew it would happen and come into my life.

Your feelings and thoughts through the force of God's Love create whether you are aware of the process or not. It gives you what you focus on, positive or negative. You then have the choice of accepting the result or tweaking it so that it becomes all that you want it to be. You are not stuck.

You need to realize that lasting happiness from the outside world is a fantasy. It can disappoint, depress, and deflate until you come to understand that happiness is the core of your being. Joy is who and what you are. God's Love gives you what It thinks you want based on your concentrated thoughts and feelings.

Certainly, you can partake or enjoy all the things you want to do, be, and have in the world, and you can also be assured as you enjoy these things that true, real and permanent happiness is within you.

Knowing is Seeing. You do not acquire happiness and good health. Your very being is happiness and health. Happiness is realized by removing unhappiness and changing your mind!

Thoughts determine how you are feeling, and feelings determine your health and happiness. If you are not happy and healthy, it is because you are thinking negatively and believe you have no choice about what is happening.

All your thoughts are only about the past or the future. So, if you are unhappy, it is because you are thinking about something that happened in the past that made you unhappy, or you are thinking about something in the future that you believe or expect will make you unhappy.

Standing between you and everlasting happiness is a thought, only one thought that is coloring the present moment. The thought is, "I don't want this." It might be a sad thought, or an angry, frightened, disillusioned, hateful, or depressed thought. Because you believe that one unhappy thought, it casts a cloud like an incoming storm to cover the happiness that you are.

Again, this one thought is from the past or future, it is not what is present in the moment because, within the present moment, there is no thought.

Being aware of God in the present fits the definition of pleasure. The only way you replace pleasure with unhappiness is by identifying with an unhappy thought about the past or future. Change your mind.

Life is beyond simple. Everything happens "for" you, not "to" you. God through Love's creative power is in charge, and everything happens at exactly the right moment, perfect timing. It's your thoughts that mislabel things as negative or less than perfect. Rather than believing or buying into the negative thought, sit back and objectively observe that the mind is telling you about its impression of what is happening. It's basing its impressions on past or future thinking, which isn't true. It's covering up God so that negative thought remains in control.

You desire peace of mind, but what you really crave is peace from mind. Past and future limitations of thought have nothing to add or to do with the present moment, which is perfect. You don't need to do anything to be happy, but you need to stop doing what makes you unhappy.

Imagine two people sitting in a doctor's office, and they hear the nurse say to the receptionist, "One of our patients coming in today is going to get a tough diagnosis."

Patient A's body immediately stiffens as his mind fills with dread and fear. His mind gets busy: What will I do if it is me? Maybe I won't be able to work. I'll have huge medical bills. Geez, I won't be able to pay my other bills either. I could lose my car. My house.

All of those negative thoughts come from attachment to his health and harboring a fear that it may deteriorate.

On the other hand, Patient B has a different reaction. He knows things in life are always changing and everything happens for the best, even if it isn't recognized at the time. He's aware that when something unexpected happens, something even better is coming. If for some reason, he gets the tough diagnosis, he knows he will handle it positively and do what needs to be done, knowing it will have a positive outcome and, in some way, he will be better for it.

Who is happier? Who is likely to have a better life? Who is drawing positivity to him? We receive what we give out, and we are moved along and affected by it.

In the case of attachment to health, the attachment comes from believing in or perhaps knowing a lack of health, that the body will fail to support you with good health and, in doing so, it can start falling apart, disease will set in, body parts will fail, it weakens so one breakdown in health will add to another. The belief in a lack of health or poor health justifies the attachment and puts your health in extreme jeopardy because everything in the body is changing all the time. Cells change, die, and are replaced and are affected by your positive or negative thinking and expectations.

Often what you are attached to makes up the identity of the person you think you are. That leads to a fear that if you drop your attachments, you will lose your identity and physical form of who you see yourself to be. All along, that attachment has robbed you of health and happiness.

When you have some illness or infirmity, think how often that subject comes to mind or is injected into your conversations. “I feel terrible.” “It hurts to move.” “I was out of work three days last week.” “First one tooth hurts, then another.” “The pain crawls up my leg.” “First it was my eyes, and now my hearing.” “I lost 10 pounds.” “I can’t keep anything down.” “I doubt my hair will ever grow back.” “My head hurts so bad I can’t think.” “My skin is so dry it feels like it is cracking.” “My tastes have changed.” “Nothing tastes good.” “Every muscle in my body hurts.” “My back hurts so bad I can’t stand up straight.”

You can be married to your unhealthy thoughts, so much so that you never think of divorcing them, and, until you make the separation, you will blindly be attached to an aging, deteriorating physical body and an unhappy life.

Henry Ford said, “Whether you think you can, or you think you can’t, you’re right.”

I mentioned earlier about my early trials in life and then my five-year bout with cancer and how I projected a challenge with my cocky attitude: “I’ve already shown I can handle anything life throws my way. Bring it on!”

It is important to recognize and analyze symptoms. Are they mental, emotional or physical? A swollen belly happening over three days, so clothes didn’t fit, was my first symptom associated with cancer. It wasn’t emotional or mental. I went to the doctor to get checked out.

I shake my head now thinking about it. My family knew I was

going through treatment, of course, but I didn't talk about it to anyone else. I worked from home and didn't miss work. I brought my laptop to the treatment center. I took chemo through a chest port one day, a belly port the next day, then the following day, got injections that worked to help build me up to do it all again the next week. After a few weeks, if I didn't bounce back, I would need blood transfusions.

It wasn't long after cancer number two of the five that my husband Jack was diagnosed with dementia, and I was his caregiver.

If I had ever been asked, I might have denied that the negative or abusive events early in my life had defined who I had become. I didn't talk about my negative early life experiences or carry them around like baggage that periodically popped open to be emotionally felt and then stuffed back in. But those events and others caused a hardening, a defiance, and an attitude that I was strong enough to handle anything tossed my way. Overall, I was happy and positive, but I mentally created challenges to prove to myself that I was strong and tough enough to take on anything life wanted to chuck my way. As mentioned earlier, I was like a wrestler who thrived on winning the match.

Being a positive-speaking, strong, dependable person was who I was on the outside, and on the inside, I mentally dared anyone to prove that wasn't true. I was up for and perhaps needed the challenge to prove to myself that I was still strong.

Carrying around emotional stuff can be hidden in so many ways. For some of us, the hurt and scars are obvious. We wear them like flashy jewelry that we want people to notice. For others, one event can cause another to periodically surface. Still for others, their past has defined them as shy, intimidated, passive people, who don't want to be noticed. Still others wear a steel cloak of bravado.

When I realized, I wasn't really who I thought I was and

pretended to be, I changed my attitude to one based on gratitude. I am grateful for health, love, happiness, ease, contentment, the ability to help others, to instantly forgive, to teach option trading, and experience fun. I say thank you dozens of times a day.

Your life, your upbringing, your religious beliefs, and your mind can become deeply attached to a myriad of fixed ideas. It is ironic that these attachments that you perhaps cling to as if they are reassurances, bind you to limitations, make your life heavy and suppress your pleasure and happiness.

You need to question and look deep and ask if you truly want to be healthy and happy. To be healthy and happy enough to feel joy, you may have to change your beliefs and ideas rather than cling to them. You can no longer say, "No way. I refuse to be happy unless my desires are fulfilled. My beliefs are important to me."

If you empty yourself of all your opinions and fixed ideas of how things should be, you would be aware of God because you would be free of all judgment, allowing everything in life, including your health, to be just as they are, knowing they are perfect. You would be in awe of the joy, happiness, and health that would flood through your body and heart, so much so that your life would spiral positively upwards in every way.

What is attached through your opinions and fixed ideas are not you, it is your mind. Attachments strengthen the mind and keep you trapped in the belief that you are small, limited, separate, one of billions, insignificant in the whole scheme of things. Or you can loosen attachments to know with certainty that you are God created through expressed Love and are unlimited and blissfully happy.

Because attachments are created by the mind, you are sometimes profoundly afraid when something the mind is attached to is threatened or taken away. Without realizing it, your mind has traded your lasting, eternal happiness for attachments. Personal identity is the greatest attachment your mind clings to. Your self-esteem and self-importance are minuscule when compared to self-worth, the God that you are.

Although you can desire, ask for, be thankful for anything you want, the problem comes when you become attached to these things and then dread and fear their loss. This is what is projected though your creative expression of God's Love, sensing it is what you want because of your intense focus on the emotions of dread and loss.

Attachment comes from believing and identifying with the mind. You can free yourself of attachments by being aware and staying as God as often as you can. One-by-one, the attachments will float away. When you're not ruled by attachments, life is freeing, incredibly joyful. Your "live in the moment" goal, the love you feel for everyone, and everything is much deeper; the appreciation and gratitude for your body and health is immeasurable. At the same time, when something changes or ends, you don't feel unbearable sadness or stress or panic because you know it's all part of God. You come to a point where you don't mind what happens. Non-attachment is your true nature. It is you, as God.

God is love, and love is the opposite of attachment. Love grants everything. The freedom to flow, to come and go. Love is accepting of everything, no matter what happens. Love is complete as it is. It doesn't want, It doesn't need, It has no shoulds or shouldn'ts. It's perfection as it is, unconditional and whole.

Ideally, you will strive to experience life as it flows in an ever-present moment, unaffected by what happens. Think of a mirror that has something ugly placed in front of it. In a sense, it absorbs the reflection but is unaffected by it. The mirror remains the mirror, and, when the ugly item is removed, the mirror is again pure and able to reflect beauty. It is open and available to absorb the image of whatever comes next. The mirror remains its pure essence no matter what happens, and it will continue that purity when a beautiful item is removed as well.

This purity is love. Truly, when you leave this earthly life, what remains and what you bring with you is the love you have expressed and shared. Love colors your essence with rainbow colors like a prism and it is what you shared to linger with others.

Within life, love is the only lasting legacy you leave behind for others. Only love is real. Love is God expressed through God's Love. The only time you can express love is in the current moment—the present—now. Love can't happen in the past or future.

Love is God, and God is Love

Love expressed through you is God and the creative energy of God's Love. It is all powerful. It is your true nature as the Spirit of God. As your attachments drop, the love you will feel will be so encompassing, it will seem as if the universe can't hold it all. All the empty places left by attachments will be filled by love that is omnipotent. This love is God.

You can be filled with love, have its freedom and happiness now. You don't have to wait for it to arrive sometime in the future when you have earned it, deserved it, or succeeded in some way that will make you ready. You have every reason and right for the happiness and joy of love to be in your life right now. There is no reason to go out and look for love; it is inside of you now. You need only to become aware and reveal it in the present moment, now.

My daughter has four chickens. This past weekend I babysat the chickens, feeding them and collecting eggs. Imagine an egg. If an egg is broken by an outside force, life ends. When an egg is broken by an inside force, life begins. Meaningful, real things always begin on the inside.

As this section wraps up, I hope that as you reflect lovingly back on your life, you can now see how your personal stories and the episodes within your life have created who you are now. Each episode helped your growth in becoming who you are, yet, in the broader view, you are God right now. You are already filled with love, whether you realize it or not. You create through God's Love thoughts. Knowing this, think only about what you truly want in your life. Believe it, know it, because Knowing is Seeing. Knowing is seeing it manifest in your life.

Points to Ponder

- Joy, abundance, peace, happiness, fun, and everything else we see as either positive or negative come from within us, not from outside ourselves.
- All that is in your life is a result of who you are and what you think; it manifests from what you pay attention to and what you want.
- If you want to bring joy and happiness into your life, look inside for those qualities because, like God, you are happiness and joy.
- If Love is God, that means God is Love, and so are, you, in God, as God.

Family

Like pieces of a puzzle, the various aspects of your identity come together to form the person you have become. This is a combination of your individual personality and God. You work, rest and play, exert energy, feel, and communicate through your body, express joy, and feel sorrow. Balance is the ultimate goal you achieve when all the aspects of your life and inner self, the Spirit of God, are in harmony. Your life force or energy flows out into the world in an expression of balance because nothing feels out of sync. While this balance is necessary to have an energetic, satisfying and joy-filled life, only you can determine what balance means to you.

A balanced life is coming to a place where you have time and energy for commitments and enjoyments, as well as time to live in a pleasurable way. With life's many levels, balance can be a difficult concept to bring into focus. Living a balanced life, however, can help you achieve a greater sense of joy, health, and satisfaction.

Jack and I were married for 53 years and have three wonderful children. When I was 40 years old, having been married 22 years at that point, my stepfather Abbott adopted me. He believed it was a life step that hadn't been handled properly when I was young, so in a sense, it was an apology. The adoption also gave me a chance to straighten out my name. I officially became Wendy L. Kirkland.

Over a lifetime, you'll encounter times when the actions of others negatively affect you. You sometimes receive an apology. At that point, you often say, "It's alright," or, "No worries. It's okay." By using that language, you are allowing, accepting, and giving permission for the same behavior to happen again. If, on the other hand, you say, "Thank you," or, "I accept your apology," you acknowledge your hurt feelings rather than ignore them.

You may decide it's easier to brush off how you really feel rather than express your discomfort over something that has happened. While at first this may seem like the best approach, what it really does is put you into a cyclical pattern of behavior. That's why it's important to recognize and end the cycle of letting someone routinely overstep your emotional boundaries. By doing this, you declare that you are a victim.

You can end this circular pattern by communicating that you

accept an apology and request for forgiveness. A simple "thank you" often is sufficient. To truly create harmony in the relationship, it helps to gently, with compassion, express your heartfelt concerns about what was said or done. By taking a deep breath and allowing God to guide your words, you can usually find the right way to share your feelings and allow the other person to realize the effect or result of what was done.

Your reply to others is important because trust and forgiveness go hand in hand. When you react in a positive way, which creates a greater amount of honesty and sincerity, you develop a more positive and empowering way of being your true self as you interact with others.

Family and friends are important, but the most vital relationship you have in your life is with yourself. When you "get right" with yourself other relationships will also become the best they can be.

Although you are the only one who is present every moment of your life, from birth onward, this inner relationship can be the most difficult one to nurture. This is true for every person. Your inner one-on-one relationship is likely a source of struggle sometimes, because societies place a great deal of emphasis on being involved with other people, first and foremost your family. Whether you're born in a city of 15 million or a village of 15, you soon experience the expectation of bonding with others. Later, a romantic relationship, even an arranged one, often implies, even in some cases, demands that you put aside your own needs for the desires and happiness of a growing number of other people. Obviously, in some societies you have wide choice, in others, children become adults with a much narrower path.

Until you know yourself, it is often hard to choose which you do support for mutual growth toward the highest goal of personal, family, and partnership potential. However, by allowing yourself to be comfortable with being alone, you can grow to become a person who can then value and participate in all types of relationships.

Early on I mentioned my family and how they helped to form who I have become. Since we are discussing family, let me share how their lives played out as it relates to me.

My dad, Reyburn, passed away soon after my eldest daughter was married. Dad came to the wedding, and that was the last time I saw him. He was bone thin as his body was shutting down from years of excessive drinking. He was never a sloppy drunk, always intellectually in control, but alcohol was close at hand, sipped throughout the day.

His second wife is now 90, and their daughter, my half-sister, is happily married with three grown children.

Abbott and my mom divorced when the twins, my youngest sisters conceived by them, were about eighteen. Mom lived in the fancy house with the pool they had designed and built together, and she rented out the four extra bedrooms to pay expenses. Starting in my teenage years, Mom drank lunchtime wine and cocktails throughout the day so sometimes she was passed out by 4:00 in the afternoon. Then she roused herself for an evening of rowdy discussion or yelling in the street if she was upset with someone as they left the house.

One evening she and a male companion went to a restaurant where she ate raw oysters. Within hours, she was in the hospital with toxic poisoning from the seafood as her body shut down because of liver disease. She passed away a few days later.

In her will, I learned she had disowned me as a daughter because, a couple of years earlier, when she and Abbott divorced, all of us kids were drawn into a hearing and interrogated by attorneys. I reluctantly answered questions, stating she often drank and sometimes was out of control if she drank too much.

The disinheritance wasn't because she had any money or possessions; disowning me was her way of cutting me out of the family. My brother and sisters felt a bit of loyalty to my mother for a while, so it took a couple years for them to decide that family, despite ups and downs, is important. Since then, we have all been very close.

Jeffrey, my brother who was paralyzed from the motor scooter accident, passed away after retiring and living a long, happy life with his wife.

Abbott (Ubee) married three other women over the years after he and Mom divorced. If he was going to be in a relationship, he believed it should be through the commitment of marriage. After the last divorce, as a single man in his 90s, he moved into a retirement building. He loved to go to their weekly dances. He always brought a cake to the event, perhaps, a day-old one from the grocery store, but he was the sweet dessert man. The older women loved him and thought he was extra special, and he liked to dance.

He passed away while having dinner at his apartment with one of my twin sisters. He leaned over and died resting his head against his daughter's shoulder.

In retrospect, it's fascinating to see how lives play out. Especially, when you can step away from having personal hang-ups and just view how various lives interplay. As it turned out, my mom and her association with the Universal Church of Ontology placed my feet on the path to discovering who I truly am as I live this happy life. And yet, she and I were estranged. This brings back thoughts of the book about the helpful angel who took on the task of being born to live a life that might need forgiveness.

Mom may well have been a messenger sent for my benefit, and it was partially on this mission that she lived her life.

The end result of this review is that you need to become personally independent and strong in your beliefs and understand who you are and why you are. Whether you are married, close to family and friends, or are living alone, it's vital to understand who you are, and, at the core of this discovery is, knowing that you are God. This means family and friends and every person you encounter in your life are all also God.

Perhaps, at no other time has it been easier for people to survive, and even thrive, while living alone. You can now support yourself financially, intermingle socially, and be healthy emotionally without needing a partner or spouse to prosper in all these areas. With this independence, you can take up your own interests, hobbies, have friends, your own business endeavors, travel, own a home, have neighbors and be a part of a community. You can take care of your own needs and develop a support system with friends, family, or a partner. You can then share the joy you have created and the beauty you have realized within yourself.

Taking time to discover, come to know and love yourself, and to find what truly makes you happy, and helps you appreciate yourself, and strengthen your commitments, gives you a certain edge. In a place of knowing, you draw in and choose people with whom to share your feelings. You decide where and to whom to commit your energy. These occasions can be with family members, friends, or a partner. Giving yourself time to enjoy being alone allows you to fully discover your most important connection, the one you have with yourself as God.

By making a mindful effort to give yourself the same support, forgiveness, love, and patience that you offer a friend, it's likely you'll be cheerful and confident most of the time.

It comes down to treating yourself the way you'd treat others, which in turn helps you avoid participating in self-defeating behaviors that can inhibit your goals. Early on, it can be an ongoing struggle to oust negative thoughts but doing so opens up vast opportunities. To think positively, you view your future plans as true realities instead of pipe dreams. Efforts you make to support your desire, and goals help you achieve a greater sense of confidence. In this way, you'll move away from self-criticism and into personal acknowledgement and respect.

Internally filled with joy, satisfaction, and peace, you are then able to settle back and maintain objectivity when it comes to accepting family and friends. Every person makes choices, and you can both accept others and maintain your personal protective boundaries by not taking part in negativity they choose. They, too, may discover who they really are and then choose a different path.

As often as you can, focus on the holiness of every person you encounter. When you pass someone on the street, send them a silent blessing. When you speak to someone at a store or anywhere else that you find yourself, know that you are speaking to God, whether that person knows it or not. This is, in fact, literally true because God is in every one of us. You won't learn that we are all the same until you see God in others. Therefore, even if it's for just a few moments each day, give the gift you'd like to receive. The gift of knowing that you are God.

Family members are often the people you will often have the hardest time acknowledging as aspects of God. You know them too well. You have lived in the same home with them and witnessed all the elements of their personalities. You've been affected by their personal choices. Through your connections with family, you may have had to suffer or witness pain, cruelty, meanness, persecution, hurt, discrimination and judgment, fighting and arguments, anger and aggression or abuse of all kinds. It's with family, usually, that you have your first brushes with rejection, neglect, belittling, selfishness, abandonment, criticism, unfairness, favoritism, teasing, and ridicule.

Of course, these experiences are usually, but not always, mingled with love, appreciation, nurturing, support, kindness, acceptance, and so on. The list could go on and on, and often you experience some things from both lists from the same person. It's complicated.

You can usually find ways to reach family reconciliation, understanding, acceptance, and perhaps even gratitude. One way to understand your past family relationships is to approach them like Neale Donald Walsch does in his children's book Little Soul and the Sun, in which the angel asked another angel to come to Earth to help them have an experience where they would learn forgiveness. Try to change your internal reaction and attitude about the person or events, by thinking of the situation as a gift. Perhaps, the experience helped you develop strength or grow in some other way.

A second way to come to appreciate past events might involve using your new understanding of God to see how your past or younger lives have helped bring you to this current discovery of who you really are. That discovery supports as you accept, forgive, or be thankful, and then move on.

A third avenue might be a degree of acceptance. You really like who you are now and know that the hurtful events of the past helped you to develop into who you have become. You come to appreciate the inner strength and flexibility you've developed.

All three avenues are internal, traveled alone and result in inner personal resolution.

Relationships with family and friends often do well with open communication. They can heal loneliness and create a deep sense of belonging. We all strive to be heard, understood, appreciated, and loved. Clear interactions make this possible. You know that expressing how you feel can bring on difficulties in relationships —or at least expose them. Remembering that we are all God can help you navigate, whether everyone involved realizes who they are or not.

In your business or casual relationships, it's vital to express yourself honestly and with clarity. With family and with others, even those in your community, sincere communication requires some planning, or you risk stumbling through interactions without awareness. However, if you over plan, you could bring in too much concern, and you either end up saying nothing or you create more confusion. When you believe you must bring up issues with any other person, being calm and centered is a state in which you can reliably speak truthfully and be kind in your response.

You can also mentally practice a few positive words to guide a healthy and beneficial conversation. The key is to have ways to center yourself, so you communicate clearly and with love. In this way, you honor the other person and create relationships in which there is a true sense of respect.

The personal relationships you form throughout your life create the comfort zone that gives you the confidence to open yourself to new experiences. Your loved ones and close friends play an important role that goes beyond offering reassurance and aid in times of crisis. They provide supportive, yet critical spaces to share your ideas and plans, and receive support when you're unsure of yourself, and lend support in return. The steadfast acceptance of these special people gently pushes you out of your comfort zone by inspiring you to push through your mental and physical borders. Every time a friend or family member helps you conquer a challenge your bond deepens and your excitement for the idea or project expands and grows stronger. The security within the personal relationships you build will help you move out of your comfort zones and stretch your self-imposed limited boundaries.

Remember, the power of God is within you, within all of us!

It's important to experience, not just believe, that you are truly one with God, and, therefore, God's creative power through God's Love is yours. You must know this to be true. This is the feeling you need to strive for and want to nurture. God did not create the world you perceive. "You" created it through the creative power of God that you share with everyone else. You possess more power than you know, and now is the time to become conscious of it.

I cannot emphasize passionately enough that you have the power to create the life and the world you want. Love expressed through God's Love is pure creativeness. It's about knowing as God knows and loving as God loves. Miracles will then flow and surround you like the scent of nature's most fragrant flower. You will then understand the reason you were born and why you exist.

QUESTIONS TO CONSIDER

1. Review the Eight Steps to Perfect Health and pick one to put into practice.
2. Do a quick self-inventory. Overall, what are three areas your health is suffering (i.e. sleep, eating habits, exercise)?
3. Identify three obstacles preventing you from improving your health. What actions can you take to overcome these obstacles?

Summary: Questions I Hope This Book Answered

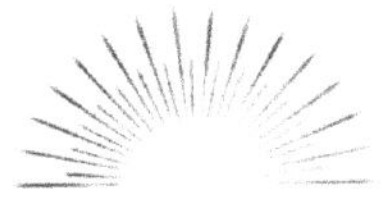

Watch or pay attention to what you tell yourself. If you continually say you can't, you prove yourself to be right. You can't. Knowing this, confirm what you truly want to happen in your life. Expect the best!

The Four Fundamental Questions of Life

1. Who am I?
2. Where am I?
3. Why am I where I am?
4. What happens next?

As I wrap up the concepts I shared, I'd like to take a moment to continue speaking directly to you as a friend.

Pause for a moment to look at the life story you have created and continue to create on an ongoing basis. If you feel comfortable about the past or how you have now embraced it and trust in your ability to handle whatever comes your way, then you are handling your life perfectly and in a manner that will serve you well. On the other hand, if you hold on to a great deal of guilt or resentment and often feel off balance in your current life, you may want to start telling yourself a new version of past and present events.

No matter who is in your story or what they have done, you are the only one who can give their involvement meaning relevant to you. You're the only one who can define what role you'll play in your own life story. By taking responsibility for the self-creating details, you will learn and grow, forgive and find compassion, and most importantly, move on into a brighter future.

From now on, you can choose to live a life story that supports you and who you really are and who you want to be. Let it be proof of your own strength, spirit, and creativity. Be kind in valuing the roles you give to yourself and generous with how many chances you get to learn what you need to know.

God has no hands but our hands, no eyes but our eyes, and no legs but our legs. When you remember and remind yourself that you are God and are the author of your own story, you then create a masterpiece because Knowing is Seeing!

Tools: Gratitude and Prosperity Affirmations

Attitudes of Gratitude and Prosperity help to reinforce inner knowing. Select one of these thoughts from my book or my personal philosophy each week and repeat several times a day for the next seven days! Internalize these knowing(s) and make them your own.

- A part of the abundance process is letting go, which creates space to receive.
- As you shine your light, everything around you is illuminated.
- Be the reason someone smiles today.
- Being thankful is one of the strongest and most transforming states of being. It shifts your perspective from lack to abundance and allows you to focus on the good in your life, which in turn pulls more blessings into your reality.
- Consider this. You attract what you know you deserve.
- Did you know Honeybees flap their wings 230 times a second? They fly 15 miles an hour and makes ½ a

teaspoon of honey in her lifetime. It's a wondrous, amazing world.

- Every day, I discover ways to love my life more.
- Everything in my life is working out for my highest good.
- Figure out what you love and do it. Love what you do, and with all your heart give yourself to that love.
- I accept that I am an unlimited human being, and I create anything and everything I desire.
- I allow my energy and mindset to attract abundance in beautiful and creative ways.
- I am a magnet for abundance. Prosperity of every type is drawn to me.
- I am growing. My possibilities are endless.
- I am in exactly the right place, attracting the right people and life is getting better and better every day.
- I am making space for more success and abundance to come into my life.
- I am open and ready to receive miracles every day.
- I am ready for prosperity in all its forms beyond my wildest dreams.
- I believe in an abundance of unlimited possibilities!
- I believe in myself and my ability to succeed.
- I choose to see the positive in every challenge.
- I deserve abundance in all areas of my life. I dwell in the midst of infinite abundance and love.
- I know God, a Spiritual Core, is within me. Therefore, I create my life.
- I know I am divinely guided, and I am moving into alignment with my soul's purpose.
- I know myself to be a generous giver and an excellent receiver.

- I make a difference everyday by knowing who I am, showing up and doing my best.
- I possess the ability to lead and inspire.
- I realize I have the power to help people through my abundance, so I stay abundant in all ways.
- If you continually say you can't, you prove yourself to be right. You can't.
- If your plan doesn't work, then change the plan, not the goal. You have to believe and then know to achieve.
- Know and understand that falling down is part of life; getting back up is living.
- Knowing is Seeing. Not the other way around.
- My life is rich with opportunities.
- My work fulfills my life and allows me to prosper.
- Pay no attention to the people who aren't happy for you, it is likely they aren't happy for themselves either. You are great!
- Surround yourself with a joyful atmosphere, created by people who talk about vision and ideas, not who talk about other people.
- Surround yourself with people who believe in your dreams, encourage your ideas, support your ambitions, and bring out the best in you.
- The comeback is always stronger and more positive than the setback.
- The only way to discover the limits of the possible is to venture a little way past them into the impossible. Which proves there are no limits.
- Think the thought until you know it. Once you know it, it will happen or come into your life.
- When you focus on being a blessing to others, God

makes sure you are always blessed in abundance, so you continue sharing.
- You are more than strong enough to face it all, even if it doesn't feel like it now.

These are some of my favorite quotes from like-minded writers and speakers, curated from a variety of sources.

- Abundance is about being rich, with or without money. - Suze Orman
- Abundance is not something we acquire. It is something we tune into. - Wayne Dyer
- Always leave enough time in your life to do something that makes you happy, satisfied, even joyous. That has more of an effect on economic well—being than any other single factor. - Paul Hawken
- Any time you start a sentence with – I AM – you are creating what you are and what you want to be. – Dr. Wayne Dyer
- Attitude is a choice. Happiness is a choice. Optimism is a choice. Kindness is a choice. Giving is a choice. Respect is a choice. Whatever choice you make makes you. Choose wisely. - Roy T. Bennett
- Be grateful for what you already have while you pursue your goals. If you aren't grateful for what you already have, what makes you think you would be happy with more. - Roy T. Bennett
- Be the change that you wish to see in the world. - Mahatma Gandhi
- Believe in your infinite potential. Your only limitations are those you set upon yourself. - Roy T. Bennett
- Believe in yourself. You are braver than you think,

more talented than you know, and capable of more than you imagine. - Roy T. Bennett

- Create a life you can't wait to wake up to. - Unknown
- Cry. Forgive. Learn. Move on. Let your tears water the seeds of your future happiness. - Steve Maraboli
- Dear Self, when you start taking care of yourself, you start feeling better. You start looking better. You start to attract better. It all starts with you. - Unknown
- Do not let the memories of your past limit the potential of your future. There are no limits to what you can achieve on your journey through life, except in your mind. - Roy T. Bennett
- Doing what you love is the cornerstone of having abundance in your life. - Wayne Dyer
- Don't be pushed around by the fears in your mind. Be led by the dreams in your heart. - Roy T. Bennett
- Enthusiasm is the yeast that raises the dough. - Paul J. Meyer
- Focus on the step in front of you, not the whole staircase. - Unknown
- Happiness is not the absence of problems; it's the ability to deal with them. - Steve Maraboli
- I am Kind - I am Brave - I am Loved - I am Strong - I am Creative - I am Grateful - I am Abundant - Unknown
- I aspire to be a giver, a giver of love, a giver of support, a giver of smiles. - Unknown
- I expect the unexpected and I expect it to be great. - Abbott (Ubee) Lieberman
- I learned a long time ago the wisest thing I can do is to be on my own side. - Maya Angelou
- If you have a strong purpose in life, you don't have to

be pushed. Your passion will drive you there. - Roy T. Bennett

- If you stumble, make it part of the dance. - Unknown
- Just as you may not be aware of the complexities of the way your body works to allow you to open that refrigerator door without thought, so the Universe has provided you with everything in abundance, allowing a continuous flow of prosperity to come your way. Only when you accept that it is possible and believe it, will you live the life that you dream about. - Zeeshan Raza
- Let the improvement of yourself keep you so busy that you have no time to criticize others. - Roy T. Bennett
- Life is about accepting the challenges along the way, choosing to keep moving forward, and savoring the journey. - Roy T. Bennett
- Live the Life of Your Dreams: Be brave enough to live the life of your dreams according to your vision and purpose instead of the expectations and opinions of others. - Roy T. Bennett
- Manifesting happens every day whether we want it to or not, we are always attracting things and people to us. The absolute key to Manifesting without missing a mark, is to do so with confident intention and complete awareness. - Sereda Aleta Dailey
- My ability to conquer my challenges is limitless; my potential to succeed is limitless. - Live With Purpose
- Never doubt that a small group of thoughtful, committed, citizens can change the world. Indeed, it is the only thing that ever has. - Margaret Mead
- Not all storms come to disrupt your life, some come to clear your path. - Unknown

- Old ways won't open new doors. - Unknown
- Once you realize you deserve a bright future, letting go of your dark past is the best choice you will ever make. - Roy T. Bennett
- Pursue what catches your heart, not what catches your eyes. - Roy T. Bennett
- Reality is a projection of your thoughts or the things you habitually think about. - Unknown
- Spirituality is like a thin-thin thread that if delicately followed guides us from darkness to light, from poverty to abundance and from destruction to safety. - Bryant McGill
- Start the habit of asking yourself: Does this support the life I am trying to create? -Unknown
- Stop trying to calm the storm. Calm Yourself. The storm will pass. - Unknown
- Stretch. It's only after you've stepped outside your comfort zone that you begin to change, grow, and transform. - Roy T. Bennett
- The key to abundance is meeting limited circumstances with unlimited thoughts. - Marianne Williamson
- The man who moves a mountain begins by carrying away small stones. - Confucius
- The purpose of life is a life of purpose. - Robin Sharma
- The Universe is always speaking to us… sending us little messages, causing coincidences and serendipities, reminding us to stop, to look around, to believe in something else, something more. - Nancy Thayer
- The wealth and abundance we seek already awaits us; it is just waiting to be collected. - Eleesha

- There is a realm in which miracles are possible and do take place. The door to this realm is the belief in all possibilities and YOU are the key. - Vivian Amis
- What if … everything you are going through is preparing you for what you asked for? - Unknown
- What's done is done. What's gone is gone. One of life's lessons is always moving on. It's okay to look back to see how far you've come but keep moving forward. - Roy T. Bennett
- When you can't control what's happening, challenge yourself to control the way you respond. That is where your power is. - Kaitlyn Moorhead
- When you can't find sunshine, be the sunshine. - Unknown
- When you recognize the many types of abundance in your life, more abundance will flow to you through all levels of your life and amongst all of the people in your life. - Cheryl Hamada
- Without darkness, we may never know how bright the stars shine. Without battles, we could not know what victory feels like. Without adversity, we may never appreciate the abundance in our lives. Be thankful, not only for the easy times, but for every experience that has made you who you are. - Julie-Anne
- You can add up your blessings or add up your troubles. Either way, you'll find you have an abundance. - Richelle E. Goodrich
- You can become instantly successful with a simple thought, but long-lasting and pronounced success comes to those who renew their commitment to a mindset of abundance every minute of every hour of every day. - Bryant McGill

- You never change your life until you step out of your comfort zone; change begins at the end of your comfort zone. - Roy T. Bennett
- You simply will not be the same person two months from now after consciously giving thanks each day for the abundance that exists in your life. - Sarah Ban Breathnach

Additional Resources: Other Authors, Teachers, Speakers

If this book has energized and inspired you to continue your journey of self-discovery and personal growth, explore these additional sources. (Listed in Alphabetical Order)

Sailor Bob Adamson
Millie America
Julian Barbour
David Bingham
Rhonda Byrne
Deepak Chopra, M.D., FACP
Anthony De Mello, S.J.
Hale Dwoskin
Peter Dziuban
Jan Frazier
Jon Gabriel
Joel Goldsmith
Chelan Harkin
Dr. David Hawkins, M.D., PH. D
Michael James

Byron Katie
Loch Kelly
Crystal "Teddy" Key
Sara Landon
Frances Rae Key
J. Krishnamurti
Dr. Robert Lanza, M.D.
Peter Lawry and Kalyani Lawry
Lester Levenson
Francis Lucille
Jac O'Keeffe
Suze Orman
Max Planck
Sri Poonja
Rumi
Peter Russell
Seneca
Rupert Spira
Eckhart Tolle
Neale Donald Walsch
Alan Watts
Erin Werley
Pamela Wilson
Paramahansa Yogananda

About the Author

Wendy Kirkland has been sharing her signature philosophy of positive expectations, thinking and the power of personal belief in creating amazing, miraculous outcomes in each of our lives for many years. Earlier she had a hard life and discovered the secrets to bring about major life changes, health and abundance and now strives to share this knowledge and understanding with others.

www.ingramcontent.com/pod-product-compliance
Lightning Source LLC
LaVergne TN
LVHW050538160826
845677LV00011B/2091

* 9 7 9 8 2 3 0 7 9 8 2 5 5 *